S.S.F. Public Library
Grand Ave.
306 Walnut Ave.
South San Francisco, CA 9408

South San Francisco Public Library

3 9048 10740131 1

D0127637

R 1

5-INGREDIENT
INSTANT POT®
COOKBOOK

S.S.F. Public Library
Grand Ave.
306 Walnut Ave.
South San Francisco, CA 94080

Authorized by Instant Pot®

5-INGREDIENT INSTANT POT® COOKBOOK

150 EASY, QUICK & DELICIOUS RECIPES

MARILYN HAUGEN

Robert
ROSE

5-Ingredient Instant Pot® Cookbook
Text copyright © 2018 Marilyn Haugen
Photographs copyright © 2018 Robert Rose Inc.
Cover and text design copyright © 2018 Robert Rose Inc.

INSTANT POT® and associated logos are owned by Double Insight Inc. Used under license. Use of the trademarks is authorized by DOUBLE INSIGHT Inc., owner of Instant Pot®.

No part of this publication may be reproduced, stored in a retrieval system or transmitted, in any form or by any means, without the prior written consent of the publisher or a license from the Canadian Copyright Licensing Agency (Access Copyright). For an Access Copyright license, visit www.accesscopyright.ca or call toll-free: 1-800-893-5777.

For complete cataloguing information, see page 192.

Disclaimer
The recipes in this book have been carefully tested by our kitchen and our tasters. To the best of our knowledge, they are safe and nutritious for ordinary use and users. For those people with food or other allergies, or who have special food requirements or health issues, please read the suggested contents of each recipe carefully and determine whether or not they may create a problem for you. All recipes are used at the risk of the consumer. Consumers should always consult their Instant Pot® manual for recommended procedures and cooking times.

We cannot be responsible for any hazards, loss or damage that may occur as a result of any recipe use.

For those with special needs, allergies, requirements or health problems, in the event of any doubt, please contact your medical adviser prior to the use of any recipe.

Design and production: Alicia McCarthy/PageWave Graphics Inc.
Editor: Sue Sumeraj
Recipe editor: Jennifer MacKenzie
Proofreader: Kelly Jones
Indexer: Gillian Watts
Photographer: Tango Photography
Food stylist: Éric Régimbald
Prop stylist: Véronique Gagnon-Lalanne

Illustrations (page 13): Kveta/threeinabox.com

Cover image: Herbed Salmon with Asparagus (page 114) and Simple Rice Pilaf (page 33)

Published by Robert Rose Inc.
120 Eglinton Avenue East, Suite 800, Toronto, Ontario, Canada M4P 1E2
Tel: (416) 322-6552 Fax: (416) 322-6936
www.robertrose.ca

Printed and bound in Canada

2 3 4 5 6 7 8 9 MI 26 25 24 23 22 21 20 19

CONTENTS

With the Instant Pot and this cookbook, you will be able to quickly and easily put together meals for any time of the day using only five ingredients, many of which are pantry staples.

PREFACE

THIS IS THE second cookbook I have been fortunate enough to write using the Instant Pot, and my third using a multicooker. And why not? The more I use it, the more scrumptious recipes I develop. The Instant Pot is a fantastic kitchen appliance that is so versatile and so incredibly easy to use, it's no wonder it has become the hottest small appliance on the market today.

The Instant Pot has many different functions, including pressure cooking, slow cooking, sautéing, yogurt-making and a whole range of push-button cooking options. This book emphasizes pressure cooking because that is how many people are looking to cook when they purchase an Instant Pot. But some of my recipes also give you the option of slow cooking instead. The sauté program is also used often throughout this collection, as browning or simmering ingredients with this function helps to improve the quality of many dishes. And I made sure to include a yogurt recipe for those of you who want to try your hand at that!

With the Instant Pot and this cookbook, you will be able to quickly and easily put together meals for any time of the day using only five ingredients, many of which are pantry staples. How easy is that? The recipes are perfect for singles, empty nesters, families, busy people, students and anyone who just wants a tasty meal with no hassle. There are even great recipes that you can make ahead, and complete meals made in one pot.

Every recipe has been tested by me, approved by my taste-testers and reviewed by experts on cooking and nutrition, so you know that the dishes will turn out well.

If you enjoy the recipes and tips in this book, stop by my blog, www.FoodThymes.com, to check out some of my other cookbooks and recipes for preparing quick, easy and healthy meals.

I am thrilled that you're joining me in the fun of Instant Pot cooking!

— MARILYN HAUGEN

ACKNOWLEDGMENTS

FOR THE TWO fabulous bookends of my life: my mom and my daughter, Natalie. The times spent cooking, eating, drinking and entertaining with you have been the best of times and have inspired my love of cooking.

My sincere appreciation to Bob Dees, my publisher, who gave me the opportunity to create this cookbook to share with you. My editor, Sue Sumeraj, is always outstanding to work with and has extraordinary insight into what will make a great experience for our readers. Sue and Jennifer MacKenzie, a recipe developer, editor and author, gave me exceptional input for this book, so you can be sure the recipes are easy to understand and will turn out as intended.

Many thanks to Alicia McCarthy of PageWave Graphics for the wonderful design; to the team at Tango Photography for the stunning photographs; and to all of the outstanding professionals at Robert Rose who make the book-creation process a truly enjoyable and successful experience.

GETTING TO KNOW THE INSTANT POT

IF YOU ARE looking for a way to get delicious, nutritious meals on the table more quickly and easily, then the Instant Pot is for you. This appliance allows you to prepare a meal with little effort or hands-on time, consistently delicious results and minimal cleanup.

So how could it possibly get any simpler? Well, it can! The recipes in this cookbook use only five ingredients that are readily available at the grocery store. You probably already have a lot of them on hand, in your fridge, freezer or pantry.

Salt, pepper, cooking oil, butter, water and broth
or stock are what I call freebies and, in this book,
are not included in the five-ingredient count.

USING YOUR INSTANT POT

When you first start using your Instant Pot, do not be intimidated by all the cooking program keys, the operation keys and the LCD display. The core uses for today's Instant Pot are pressure cooking, sautéing, slow cooking and making yogurt. The remaining program keys you see also use the pressure cooking function, but are preprogrammed to high or low pressure and the recommended cooking time. You can use these programs, if you prefer, and adjust the time to what is stated in the recipe.

As of this writing, the USDA has not tested the Instant Pot
for canning purposes. Refer to the USDA's *Complete Guide to
Home Canning* for more information on safe canning methods.

There are several Instant Pot models available, and different models have different cooking programs. Refer to the user manual that came with your appliance for a more detailed explanation of its programs. In recent models, there are seven core functions:

Core Instant Pot Functions

- Pressure cooking (with keys including Pressure Cook or Manual Pressure, Soup/Broth, Meat/Stew, Bean/Chili, Rice, Multigrain, Porridge, Steam, Cake and Egg)
- Slow cooking
- Sautéing
- Yogurt-making (including subprograms for making yogurt, pasteurizing milk and making jiuniang)
- Sterilizing (see canning sidebar)
- Keeping food warm
- Delaying the start of cooking (when using this function, make sure the ingredients you are using are safe to stand at room temperature until cooking begins)

In addition to the cooking programs, there are operations keys that enable you to adjust the pressure, temperature and cooking time of some programs. Each recipe will tell you what adjustments you need to make for that recipe. Keep in mind that it is very important to follow the steps exactly as written to ensure that you get the best results, safely and mess-free. Consult your user manual for instructions on how to make the necessary adjustments to pressure, temperature and cooking time for each program.

....

Some newer Instant Pot models use a dial, rather than push buttons, to select the cooking program.

....

On the following pages, you'll find some additional tips for success with your Instant Pot, whether you are following one of the recipes in this book or venturing out on your own.

PRESSURE COOKING

- In some Instant Pot models, the pressure cooking function is labeled Pressure Cook; in others, it is labeled Manual (for manual pressure) instead.
- You must have a minimum of 1 cup (250 mL) liquid in the pot. Check the user manual for your specific model for the amount of liquid needed to bring your pot to pressure. Many of the recipes call for 1 cup (250 mL) water to be added to the pot; if your model requires more liquid, increase the amount of water as necessary. In other recipes, there is sufficient liquid from other ingredients to meet at least the minimum requirements without the addition of 1 cup (250 mL) water.

- The cooker must be no more than two-thirds full for any recipe, and no more than half full for ingredients, such as beans and grains, that may foam or expand during cooking.

After cooking thicker and stickier foods, such as beans or grains, or foods high in fat, take extra care when opening the lid, as these foods may bubble and spurt out.

- Some Instant Pot models have High and Low Pressure options, some use only High Pressure, and others include Custom options. Follow the recipe instructions for choosing the pressure level. If the recipe uses Low Pressure and your model does not have that setting, you can cut the cooking time in half and use High Pressure, checking the food for doneness as per the instructions in the recipe. You may need to experiment a bit with cooking times, and the results may not be as intended.

The actual cooking time does not start until after working pressure is reached, which can take about 10 to 20 minutes, depending on the volume and temperature of ingredients in the pot.

Releasing Pressure

- **Quick Release:** When the cooking time is done, press Cancel and turn the steam release handle to Venting. This immediately releases all of the pressure in the pot and stops the cooking process. When the float valve drops down, you will be able to open the lid. Keep your hands and face away from the hole on the top of the steam release handle so you don't get scalded by the escaping steam. You may want to use an oven mitt when turning the handle. Never cover the steam release handle with a towel or any other item that catches the releasing steam.

The type of pressure release used in a recipe can increase the overall cooking time. While pressure cooking is a faster cooking method, the time the appliance takes to come to pressure and to release pressure should be accounted for when you are planning your meals.

- **10-Minute Release:** When the cooking time is done, press Cancel and let the pot stand, covered, for 10 minutes. After 10 minutes, turn the steam release handle to Venting, wait for the float valve to drop down, then remove the lid. This release method is often used for dishes that benefit from an additional 10 minutes in the cooker's steam. (Occasionally, recipes may call for more or less standing time.)
- **Natural Release:** When the cooking time is done, press Cancel and let the pot stand, covered, until the float valve drops down. Turn the steam release handle to Venting, as a precaution, and remove the lid. This release method can take about 15 to 25 minutes, depending on the volume of ingredients and the pressure level. It is used for dishes that foam and could cause clogging of the exhaust valve or spewing of ingredients out through the exhaust valve. It is also used for certain dishes that benefit from the additional standing time. This release method may be called NPR (natural pressure release) in other cookbooks and in recipes online.

Steaming

- Many of the recipes in this book use the Pressure Cook or Manual function to steam food, either directly on a steam rack or in a steamer basket, or in a heatproof dish, bowl or pan placed on a steam rack.
- Be very careful when removing steamed items from the Instant Pot after the cooking time is done. For foods placed directly on the rack (such as eggs, peppers, potatoes, etc.), or for foods in small containers, such as silicone baking cups, custard cups or ramekins, small silicone oven mitts or silicone-coated tongs will help you remove them without burning yourself. See page 17 for more information on these tools.
- Shallow dishes and pans can be easily removed from the pot using the handles of the steam rack to lift the rack straight up out of the pot, with the dish or pan on top, and transfer it to the countertop. Make sure you still protect your hands with silicone oven mitts!
- For deeper bowls and dishes that would be difficult to remove using the steam rack handles, create a crisscross foil sling to help you get them out of the pot easily (see page 16 for more information on creating a crisscross sling).

• •

The lid must always be closed and locked and the steam release handle turned to Sealing when you are using a pressure cooking function.

• •

CREATING FOIL OR PARCHMENT PACKETS FOR STEAMING FOOD

In several of the recipes, the food is steamed inside of foil or parchment packets (en papillote) placed on the steam rack. Here's how to make the tent-style and flat packets described in the recipes:

TENT-STYLE PACKETS

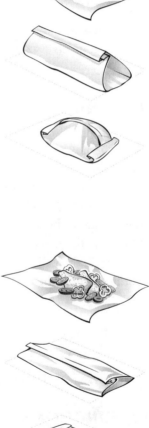

1. Place the ingredients in the center of the foil or parchment paper as directed in the recipe.
2. Bring the long ends of the foil or paper up to meet over the ingredients. Fold down the foil or paper until the top of the packet is tightly sealed but there is enough of a gap between the food and the top of the packet to allow air and steam to circulate.
3. Fold or crimp up the open ends of the foil or paper until the folds are tight against the ingredients and the packet is tightly sealed.

FLAT PACKETS

1. Place the ingredients in the center of the foil or parchment paper as directed in the recipe.
2. Bring the long ends of the foil or paper up to meet over the ingredients. Fold down the foil or paper until it is tight against the ingredients.
3. Fold up the open ends of the foil or paper until the folds are tight against the ingredients and the packet is tightly sealed.

SLOW COOKING

- Unless you are directed by a recipe to leave the lid off, the lid should be closed and locked, and the steam release handle turned to Venting, when you are using the slow cooking function.
- Fill the cooker half to three-quarters full to avoid over- or undercooking.
- Avoid removing the lid during the cooking time. Doing so releases valuable heat, which can alter the amount of cooking time your dish gets at the correct temperature. If looking at your slow-cooking dish is something you feel you must do, use the Instant Pot glass lid instead of the pressure cooking lid.
- All Instant Pot models have three temperature settings — Less, Normal and More — for slow cooking, and some have a Custom option as well. Follow the recipe instructions for the ideal setting.

Never use frozen meats when slow cooking, as your dish may never reach a safe temperature.

SAUTÉING

- The lid must always be kept off when you're sautéing or browning food. Do not even partially cover the pot with the lid, as you might do on the stovetop when simmering sauces, as pressure can build in the pot and be very dangerous.
- Always press Cancel when you are done sautéing, before moving on to other steps, such as pressure cooking or slow cooking.
- The Sauté function has three temperature settings — Less, Normal and More — in all Instant Pot models, and some have a Custom option. Follow the instructions in the recipe for the best setting.

For best results, wait to start sautéing or browning until the display says "Hot."

ALL FUNCTIONS

- Ingredients should be added in the order listed and as directed in the instructions.
- All ingredients must be added to the inner cooking pot, never directly into the cooker housing.
- Keep the steam release valve free of any obstructions. After use, make sure to clean the valve and screens.

- Keep your Instant Pot clear of any cupboards, to prevent damage from the steam release.
- Whenever you are opening the lid after cooking, tilt the lid away from you so you don't get scalded by escaping steam.
- Make sure the sealing ring inside the lid is correctly placed so that the pot has a tight seal. After many uses, you may want to replace the ring if it has lost some of its form or has picked up odors. Replace the sealing ring only with authorized Instant Pot rings.

At altitudes above 3,000 feet (914 meters), recipes will require a change in cooking time or temperature, or both. Contact your multicooker's manufacturer to learn the adjustments needed for your altitude.

RECOMMENDED ACCESSORIES

Aside from your Instant Pot and some standard kitchen utensils, there are a few other kitchen gadgets that you will need (or will find handy) when preparing the recipes in this book.

- **Standard measuring cups and spoons:** Use a glass measuring cup with a spout to measure liquids. Use nesting-style dry measuring cups to measure dry and moist ingredients. Measuring spoons can be used to measure both dry and liquid ingredients; always measure dry ingredients before wet ones so the dry ingredients don't stick to the spoon.
- **Kitchen gloves:** A pair of kitchen gloves is very useful when you're handling hot peppers, certain spices and fruits or vegetables that can stain your hands.
- **Large chef's knife:** A sharp chef's knife is the best tool for cutting meats and vegetables to fit into your Instant Pot.
- **Sieve:** A fine-mesh sieve is useful for rinsing rice and beans, and for straining liquids.
- **Electric mixer:** Either a stand mixer or a handheld mixer can be used; either make it much easier to mix ingredients for cakes and puddings.
- **Food processor:** In some recipes, you will need to process ingredients to make items such as puréed pumpkin, chopped clams or cheesecake batter.

One of my favorite kitchen gadgets is a garlic press. You can certainly mince garlic by hand, but a press makes this frequent task a snap.

- **Immersion blender or stand blender:** An immersion blender makes puréeing soups incredibly easy, as you can use it right in the pot. If you don't have an immersion blender, you will find alternative instructions for using a stand blender in a tip accompanying the recipe.

- **Ovenproof bakeware:** 4- and 6-oz (125 and 175 mL) ramekins, a 6-cup (1.5 L) round casserole dish, a 4-cup (1 L) round soufflé dish, a 6-inch (15 cm) springform pan and a 7-inch (18 cm) nonstick fluted pan (such as a Bundt or kugelhopf pan) are useful for making desserts, egg dishes and rice in your multicooker, or when cooking smaller volumes. Small or jumbo silicone baking cups are also handy.

- **8-oz (250 mL) canning jars with lids:** If you want to process yogurt in jars, these are the ones you will need for my recipes.

- **Steamer basket:** You will need a steamer basket to hold vegetables and other ingredients such as meatballs and chicken wings while steaming. If your steamer basket has legs that extend its height, it may sit high enough above the water or other ingredients in the pot; otherwise, place a steam rack in the pot and place the steamer basket on the rack.

- **Tall steam rack:** All Instant Pots come with a standard steam rack. However, you may find a taller rack useful when you're making a pot-in-pot recipe where you don't want the top layer to touch the bottom ingredients.

••

An instant-read thermometer is one of the best tools for making sure your meats and poultry are properly cooked.

••

- **Crisscross foil sling:** When you are steaming food inside a bowl or dish that fits very snugly in the pot and is deep enough that it would be difficult to use the handles of the steam rack to remove it from the pot, create a crisscross foil sling to help you lift the dish or bowl out. It's easy to make a crisscross sling. Simply fold two 18-inch (45 cm) lengths of foil lengthwise into thirds, making two strips. Crisscross the center points of the strips on the steam rack, bringing the ends of the strips up the sides of the pot and over the rim. Place the bowl or dish on the crisscrossed strips on the rack and tuck the strip ends into the pot before closing and locking the lid. When the cooking time is done, grip the strip ends to lift out the bowl or dish. These foil strips can be reused several times, so store them with your Instant Pot for easy retrieval.

- **Small silicone oven mitts:** These mitts, also called pinch mitts or mini oven mitts, are handy when lifting a hot steam basket, steam rack, baking cups or ramekins out of the pot. They are heat- and water-resistant and improve your grip on hot items you are lifting out of the pot. Look for Instant Pot mini mitts or other food-grade silicone mitts in case a mitt touches the food.
- **Silicone-coated tongs:** These will help prevent slippery ingredients from splashing back into the pot when you are turning or removing them.

THE INSTANT POT PANTRY

All of the recipes in this book use just five ingredients. Not included in the ingredient count are what I call freebies: cooking oil, butter, salt, pepper, water and broth or stock. Optional ingredients are also omitted from the ingredient count.

••

Pressure cooking requires liquid to bring the appliance up to pressure, and many of the recipes in this book use broth or stock as the necessary liquid; therefore, these ingredients were not included in the recipe count.

••

All of the ingredients are readily available in grocery stores, so shopping for ingredients will be just as easy as cooking them. As much as possible, I tried not to use processed food, but I truly felt some recipes worked better with them. In addition, many of the recipes use nonperishable items and/or frozen foods so you can cook a meal without going to the store — provided you keep your pantry and freezer well-stocked, of course!

Here are some staples, used in a large number of recipes, that you will want to be sure to keep on hand:

STOCKS AND BROTHS

Vegetable broth or stock, chicken broth or stock, and beef broth or beef bone broth are used in many of these recipes to add flavor and as a substitute for water as the liquid. You can use either homemade stock or store-bought ready-to-use broth in any of the recipes. You can also use broth prepared from bouillon cubes, but their sodium content is usually quite high, so you may want to reduce the amount of salt in the recipe.

On pages 26–28, you will find recipes and variations for both low-sodium and no-salt-added homemade stocks and broth. The recipes specify which to use depending on what will create the best flavor balance. You can certainly substitute one for the other, or even use full-sodium ready-to-use broths, but keep in mind that any change will affect the flavor balance of the dish. If you use no-salt-added stock or broth in a recipe that calls for reduced-sodium, you may want to add a bit of salt to compensate. (At least in that case you control the amount of added sodium.)

••

Using the type of stock or broth specified in the recipe will give you the best balance of flavors in the finished dish.

••

MEATS

Fresh meat is used in all of the recipes. If necessary, you can use frozen meat, but you will need to increase the cooking time. Also keep in mind that frozen meat cannot be seared before pressure cooking, which can alter the flavor of the finished dish. If you want to sear the meat, thaw it overnight in the refrigerator.

SALT AND PEPPER

Regular table salt is used unless coarse salt really contributes to making the recipe better. You can substitute kosher or sea salt for table salt, if you prefer.

Freshly ground black pepper yields much better flavor and results than pre-ground pepper, but you can use whichever you have on hand.

HERBS, SEASONINGS AND FLAVORINGS

When adding fresh or dried herbs, seasonings and flavorings, remember that a little goes a long way. Always use the amount specified in the recipe for the best flavor and consistency.

If you are confident in your cooking skills and are familiar with a recipe, you may want to adjust the type or amount of these ingredients. Make any changes in small increments, since cooking under pressure is different from stovetop or oven cooking.

••

Increase the amount of spicy ingredients with caution, as pressure cooking intensifies the spiciness of the final dish.

••

FLAVOR BASE MIXTURES

Flavor bases give recipes wonderful depth of flavor. They include very common ingredients, such as onions, celery and carrots, that are often used at the start of a recipe. When developing recipes with a limit of five ingredients, I often found myself having to choose just one or two of these fundamental ingredients that I felt added the most to the recipe. So I wanted to mention the following flavor base mixtures, which can be used as a substitution for single flavor base ingredients as desired.

Make a flavor base substitution only if you are familiar with the recipe and comfortable with your cooking skills. For example, if a stew recipe calls for 1 chopped onion, which yields about ¾ cup (175 mL), you can substitute ¾ cup (175 mL) mirepoix instead.

- **Mirepoix:** A combination of 2 parts onion, 1 part celery and 1 part carrot. For example, ¾ cup (175 mL) mirepoix would be made up of 6 tbsp (90 mL) chopped onion, 3 tbsp (45 mL) chopped celery and 3 tbsp (45 mL) chopped carrot. Mirepoix is most often used as a base in soups and stews.
- **Holy Trinity:** A combination of 3 parts onion, 2 parts celery and 1 part green bell pepper. For example, ¾ cup (175 mL) holy trinity would be made up of 6 tbsp (90 mL) chopped onion, 4 tbsp (60 mL) chopped celery and 2 tbsp (30 mL) chopped green bell pepper. This base is used in Cajun and Creole cooking.
- **Battuto:** This mixture starts with the mirepoix and adds any combination of chopped fennel, chopped fresh parsley and minced garlic in small amounts to taste. It is used primarily in Italian dishes, such as ragù Bolognese.
- **Sofrito:** A combination of 3 parts sweet onion, 3 parts bell pepper, 2 parts tomato and ½ part garlic. For example, ¾ cup (175 mL) sofrito would be made up of 4 tbsp (60 mL) chopped sweet onion, 4 tbsp (60 mL) chopped bell pepper, 8 tsp (40 mL) chopped tomato and 2 tsp (10 mL) minced garlic. This combination is used primarily in Spanish dishes, such as paella. Latin American dishes often use more garlic and add other ingredients, such as cilantro, ground cumin and other types of sweet peppers, that complement their particular cuisine.

Flavor base mixtures can be stored in an airtight container in the refrigerator for up to 3 days. Sofrito can be stored in an airtight container in the freezer for up to 3 months. Celery does not freeze well, so do not freeze flavor base mixtures with celery.

OILS

Vegetable oil and olive oil are used in many of the recipes in this book. Use your preferred type of vegetable oil. Virgin olive oil is a better (and less expensive) choice for recipes that are cooked, as it has a higher smoke point than extra virgin olive oil. The high quality and superior taste of extra virgin olive oil make it the best choice for salads and other recipes that are not cooked.

Some recipes use a slightly larger amount of oil than you may be used to. This is because the inner pot has a convex bottom and oil tends to move to the edges of the pot rather than coating the center.

Virgin coconut oil, peanut oil, sunflower oil, sesame oil, grapeseed oil and hemp oil are also good options to have on hand.

••

Nonstick cooking spray is used to coat pans and
occasionally the inner pot, to prevent sticking.

••

VINEGARS

Vinegar can impact the texture, color, flavor and thickness of dishes, adding acidity and sourness that can increase our enjoyment of our food. There are many types of vinegar, each of which has its own unique flavor. The vinegars used in this book include balsamic vinegar, apple cider vinegar and white wine vinegar. If you are unsure which ones to have on hand, start with whichever one is used in a recipe you want to make, then expand your pantry provisions from there.

SAUCES

Pasta sauce and barbecue sauce are used in several recipes. I have included recipes for homemade versions of these sauces (see pages 36–39), to use in my recipes or in any dish you like. But any ready-to-use sauce you enjoy or have on hand can be used in place of the homemade sauces.

CONDIMENTS

Versatile condiments that will add zest and flavor to your dishes include Dijon mustard, ketchup, hot pepper sauce, soy sauce, Worcestershire sauce and honey. Stock your pantry with a variety of condiments that suit your taste, as they can be used to enhance many dishes.

OTHER STAPLES

Cornstarch, brown sugar, tomato paste and vanilla extract are frequently used in these recipes, as thickeners or flavor enhancers.

••

Cornstarch should be added only after pressure cooking is completed, not at the beginning of a recipe, as you may be used to.

••

GETTING THE MOST FROM YOUR INSTANT POT

With all the wonderful dishes you can make in your Instant Pot, it's no wonder it has quickly become a favorite small kitchen appliance and has such a large and devoted fan base. Its ability to rapidly prepare a delicious meal — even with just five ingredients — while using very little counter space is sure to please new and experienced users alike.

Here are some tips on how you can make it even more useful:

- Make homemade stocks (see pages 26–28) and sauces (see pages 36–39) for use in other recipes.
- Cook dishes ahead of time and refrigerate or freeze them until ready to serve.
- On hot summery days, use your Instant Pot instead of heating up the house with your oven.
- Prepare an all-in-one meal with several different components using a steam rack and the stacking techniques described in several of the recipes in this book (see variation, page 33, or recipe, page 88, for example).
- Make a side dish, such as steamed vegetables, to accompany a main dish prepared by other methods.
- When feeding a crowd, or anytime your oven is filled to capacity, use your Instant Pot to prepare one of the dishes for your feast.

INSTANT POT BONUSES

An Instant Pot offers many benefits to the home cook, but when it comes to ingredients, two bonuses in particular stand out:

1. You can often use tougher, and therefore less expensive, cuts of meat, and they will become fork-tender in your Instant Pot.
2. You can prepare beans, rice and stocks from scratch, without any processed ingredients.

IT'S TIME TO GET FOOD ON THE TABLE!

Once you have decided on a recipe you want to prepare, scan the ingredient and equipment lists to make sure you have everything you need on hand and read the recipe all the way through before you start, to avoid unexpected surprises like necessary marinating or refrigeration time. For best results, purchase fresh meats, poultry, fish, vegetables and fruits just before you want to use them or, at the most, 2 to 3 days ahead.

You will have the most success with your dishes if you have all of the ingredients prepped and ready to go before you start following the recipe steps (unless otherwise directed in the method).

••

It's a good idea to measure out ingredients ahead of time. This is a great way to speed up your cooking and make sure you have everything ready to use when you need it.

••

QUICK TIPS FOR BEST RESULTS

- Use the manual included with your Instant Pot for a complete description of the control panel and all of the cooking programs, operation keys and indicators. The manufacturer is the expert on how to use its equipment for best results and safety.
- Measure ingredients carefully for optimal results.
- Follow the recipe steps exactly and in the order listed.
- Clean the cooker's inner pot, lid and housing according to the manufacturer's directions after each use.
- Clean the anti-block shield on the inside of the lid, the exhaust valve, the condensation collector and the sealing ring regularly to keep your cooker functioning properly.

••

Safety Note: As with any cooking appliance, parts of the Instant Pot will become very hot. Be careful when handling the inner pot and any bakeware or steaming inserts used for cooking, and always be very cautious when releasing the steam from the vent and when opening the lid.

••

CANNED OR PACKAGED SUBSTITUTIONS

Whenever possible, these recipes are intended to be from-scratch cooking. In some instances, you may want — or need — to substitute a canned or packaged alternative for the ingredient specified. If you make these types of substitutions, make sure the amount you use is equivalent to the amount of the fresh ingredient specified in the recipe. You may also need to add the ingredient at a different time in the cooking process.

Some of the recipes include tips for substituting canned or packaged ingredients in cases where the fresh ingredient may be difficult to find in certain markets or at certain times of year.

INSTANT POT STAPLES

Low-Sodium Beef Bone Broth

Homemade beef bone broth bestows a deep, rich flavor upon many dishes, adding greater depth than store-bought broth. You can also drink it, for a satisfying, nutrient-rich paleo treat. Making bone broth in the Instant Pot significantly cuts down on the preparation time.

MAKES ABOUT 8 CUPS (2 L)

COOKING PROGRAMS
• Sauté •
• Pressure Cook •

2 tbsp	vegetable oil (approx.)	30 mL
4 lbs	beef shanks, oxtails or short ribs	2 kg
2	leeks (middle green parts only), thickly sliced	2
1/2 oz	dried shiitake mushrooms	15 g
3	bay leaves	3
1 tbsp	whole black peppercorns	15 mL
8 cups	water	2 L
1 tsp	apple cider vinegar or dry red wine (optional)	5 mL

1. Set your Instant Pot to sauté on Normal. When the display says Hot, add 1 tbsp (15 mL) oil and heat until shimmering. Working in batches, add beef and cook, turning often, for 5 to 7 minutes or until browned on all sides, adding more oil as needed between batches. Using tongs, transfer beef to a plate as it is browned. Press Cancel.

2. Return all beef and any accumulated juices to the pot. Add leeks, mushrooms, bay leaves, peppercorns, water and vinegar (if using), stirring well.

3. Close and lock the lid and turn the steam release handle to Sealing. Set your Instant Pot to pressure cook on High for 90 minutes.

4. When the cooking time is done, press Cancel and let stand, covered, until the float valve drops down, then remove the lid.

5. Strain stock through a fine-mesh strainer into a large container, discarding bones and pressing on solids to extract more liquid. Discard solids.

6. To use immediately, skim fat from broth and serve. If using later, set container in a sink of ice water until broth is cool, then cover and refrigerate for at least 8 hours or overnight. Skim congealed fat from top of broth.

TIPS

The types of bones and the amount of meat on them will determine the flavor of the broth. More meat will yield a richer and more beefy broth.

After cooking the broth, you can add salt to taste, if desired. Just be aware that the beef already contributes notable amounts of sodium.

Instead of browning the beef in the pressure cooker, you can roast it in the oven. Arrange beef on a foil-lined rimmed baking sheet and drizzle with oil. Bake at 400°F (200°C) for 1 hour, turning once. Add beef and any accumulated juices to the cooker and continue with step 2.

The broth can be stored in airtight containers in the refrigerator for up to 3 days or in the freezer for up to 6 months.

Chicken Stock

Homemade chicken stock is noticeably richer than store-bought broth. Making it in the Instant Pot significantly cuts down on the preparation time, and the extracted flavors are outstanding.

MAKES ABOUT 8 CUPS (2 L)

COOKING PROGRAM

• Pressure Cook •

3 lbs	chicken wings or other parts (see tip)	1.5 kg
3	stalks celery, chopped	3
1	large onion, coarsely chopped	1
5	sprigs fresh parsley	5
2	bay leaves	2
1 tsp	salt	5 mL
8 cups	water	2 L

1. In the inner pot, combine wings, celery, onion, parsley, bay leaves, salt and water.

2. Close and lock the lid and turn the steam release handle to Sealing. Set your Instant Pot to pressure cook on High for 55 minutes.

3. When the cooking time is done, press Cancel and let stand, covered, until the float valve drops down, then remove the lid.

4. Strain stock through a fine-mesh strainer into a large container, pressing on solids to extract more liquid. Discard solids.

5. To use immediately, skim fat from stock and serve. If using later, set container in a sink of ice water until broth is cool, then cover and refrigerate for at least 8 hours or overnight. Skim congealed fat from top of stock.

VARIATIONS

Low-Sodium Chicken Stock: Reduce the salt to 1/4 tsp (1 mL).

No-Salt-Added Chicken Stock: Omit the salt. Before step 1, set your Instant Pot to sauté on Normal. When the display says Hot, add 2 tbsp (30 mL) vegetable oil and heat until shimmering. Add celery and onion; cook, stirring often, for 5 to 7 minutes or until onion is browned and celery is softened. Press Cancel and continue with step 1.

TIPS

You can use any chicken parts or bony scraps you have on hand, but parts such as wings, backs and feet will produce stocks that are much richer and thicker.

For deeper flavor, brown the chicken parts before use. Before step 1, press Sauté until Normal is highlighted. When the display says Hot, add 2 tbsp (30 mL) vegetable oil or schmaltz (rendered chicken fat) and heat until shimmering. Working in batches, add chicken parts to the pot and cook, turning often, until browned. Press Cancel and continue with step 1.

The stock can be stored in airtight containers in the refrigerator for up to 2 days or in the freezer for up to 7 months. It will gel in the refrigerator. Measure it out as directed in the recipe or reheat to liquefy.

Vegetable Stock

Homemade vegetable stock is a great way to use leftover vegetable scraps and is a wonderful replacement for chicken stock in vegetarian and vegan recipes.

MAKES ABOUT 8 CUPS (2 L)

COOKING PROGRAM

• Pressure Cook •

2	large onions, chopped	2
2	carrots, diced	2
2	stalks celery, diced	2
2	cloves garlic, smashed	2
5	sprigs fresh parsley or thyme	5
1 tbsp	whole black peppercorns	15 mL
1 tsp	salt	5 mL
8 cups	water	2 L

TIPS

Use a combination of vegetables you have on hand, but keep the onions, carrots and garlic, as they form a good foundation. You can add leftover broccoli stems, chopped celery root, corn cobs or the dark green ends of leeks for added flavor and texture and to use up leftover ingredients.

The stock can be stored in airtight containers in the refrigerator for up to 3 days or in the freezer for up to 3 months.

1. In the inner pot, combine onions, carrots, celery, garlic, parsley, peppercorns, salt and water.

2. Close and lock the lid and turn the steam release handle to Sealing. Set your Instant Pot to pressure cook on High for 15 minutes.

3. When the cooking time is done, press Cancel and let stand, covered, until the float valve drops down, then remove the lid.

4. Strain stock through a fine-mesh strainer into a large container, pressing on solids to extract more liquid. Discard solids.

5. Let stand at room temperature until cool. Cover and refrigerate for 8 hours, until chilled, before using.

VARIATIONS

Low-Sodium Vegetable Stock: Replace the salt with 2 tsp (10 mL) coconut amino acids.

No-Salt-Added Vegetable Stock: Omit the salt. Add ½ oz (15 g) dried shiitake mushrooms.

Aromatic Beans

When your recipe calls for cooked or canned beans, use this recipe as your starting point. Why buy canned beans when pressure cooking them is so quick and easy? Plan ahead, though, as you will want to soak them overnight.

MAKES ABOUT 1½ CUPS (375 ML)

COOKING PROGRAM

• Pressure Cook •

¾ cup	dried beans	175 mL
	Water	
1	clove garlic, smashed	1
1	bay leaf	1
1 tsp	vegetable oil	5 mL

1. In a large bowl, combine beans and 3 cups (750 mL) cold water. Let stand at room temperature for 8 hours or overnight. Drain and rinse.

2. Add beans, garlic, bay leaf, 1½ cups (375 mL) cold water and oil to the inner pot. Close and lock the lid and turn the steam release handle to Sealing. Set your Instant Pot to pressure cook on High and adjust the time as per your type of bean (see time chart, page 179).

3. When the cooking time is done, press Cancel and let stand, covered, until the float valve drops down, then remove the lid. The beans should be al dente. (If more cooking time is needed, continue pressure cooking on High for 2 to 5 minutes, depending on the type of bean, then quickly release the pressure.) Discard bay leaf and garlic.

4. Add beans, with or without their liquid, according to your recipe's directions. If storing beans, store them in their liquid.

VARIATIONS

Aromatic Beans and Veggies: Add up to two vegetables, such as 1 halved carrot, 2 halved celery sticks and/or 1 quartered bell pepper. You can omit the garlic or keep it in.

In place of the water in step 2, you can use store-bought ready-to-use vegetable, chicken or beef broth, or try one of the stock or broth recipes on pages 26–28.

Replace the garlic with 1 quartered onion.

Replace the bay leaf with a sprig of fresh thyme, rosemary or sage.

Replace the vegetable oil with butter or bacon fat.

TIPS

This recipe yields about the same amount of beans as a 15-oz (425 mL) can.

To make discarding herbs easier, place them in a square of fine-mesh cheesecloth and tie it tightly closed.

Quick and Easy Quinoa

Quinoa is a protein-powered grain that pairs well with nuts, vegetables, meats and other grains, or is delicious all on its own. This simple base recipe will launch many fabulous meatless mains and breakfasts, and makes the ideal side dish for fish or chicken.

MAKES 4 SERVINGS

COOKING PROGRAMS

• Sauté •
• Pressure Cook •

2 tsp	vegetable oil	10 mL
1 cup	quinoa, rinsed and well drained	250 mL
	Salt	
1½ cups	water	375 mL

TIPS

This recipe can be doubled, as long as you don't fill the pot more than halfway.

While some packages say the quinoa is already rinsed, I like to rinse it again to remove any bitter taste.

To reheat 1 serving of leftovers, microwave, stirring once, for 1 minute or until warmed through. You may need to add water, in 1-tbsp (15 mL) increments, if the mixture becomes too dry.

1. Set your Instant Pot to sauté on Normal. When the display says Hot, add oil and heat until shimmering. Add quinoa and cook, stirring, for 2 to 3 minutes or until lightly toasted and fragrant. Press Cancel. Add ¼ tsp (1 mL) salt and water, stirring well.

2. Close and lock the lid and turn the steam release handle to Sealing. Set your Instant Pot to pressure cook on High for 2 minutes.

3. When the cooking time is done, press Cancel and let stand, covered, for 10 minutes, then turn the steam release handle to Venting. When the float valve drops down, remove the lid. The quinoa should be tender. (If more cooking time is needed, continue pressure cooking on High for 0 minutes, then quickly release the pressure.)

4. Fluff quinoa with a fork and season to taste with salt. Serve immediately.

Super-Simple Brown Rice

Rice, water and an Instant Pot — it really doesn't get much simpler than that. Brown rice does take longer to cook than white rice because it retains its outer layer, called the bran, but the added nutritional benefits are worth the extra time.

MAKES 4 SERVINGS

COOKING PROGRAM

• Pressure Cook •

1⅓ cups	long- or short-grain brown rice, rinsed	325 mL
¼ tsp	salt	1 mL
1⅔ cups	water	400 mL
1 tsp	vegetable oil	5 mL

1. In the inner pot, combine rice, salt, water and oil.

2. Close and lock the lid and turn the steam release handle to Sealing. Set your Instant Pot to pressure cook on High for 18 minutes.

3. When the cooking time is done, press Cancel and let stand, covered, for 10 minutes, then turn the steam release handle to venting. When the float valve drops down, remove the lid. The rice should be tender. (If more cooking time is needed, continue pressure cooking on High for 2 minutes, then quickly release the pressure.)

4. Fluff rice with a fork. Serve immediately.

VARIATIONS

Pot-in-Pot: To cook a complete meal or another ingredient, such as vegetables in foil, at the same time, add 1 cup (250 mL) hot water to the inner pot and place a steam rack in the pot. In step 1, combine rice, salt, water and oil in a 4-cup (1 L) heatproof dish. Place the dish on the rack. Continue with step 2.

Brown Rice with Almonds and Green Onions: Stir in 4 tsp (20 mL) slivered almonds and 1 sliced green onion in step 1.

In place of the water, use ready-to-use reduced-sodium chicken or vegetable broth, Low-Sodium Chicken Stock (variation, page 27) or Low-Sodium Vegetable Stock (variation, page 28) and omit the salt.

TIP

The key to perfect rice is letting the pot stand, covered, for the recommended time before releasing the pressure. Not only does this continue gently cooking the rice, but it also prevents rice and steam from clogging the steam release valve, which might happen if the pressure is released too early.

Foolproof Jasmine Rice

Jasmine rice is a perfect accompaniment to Asian dishes, especially Thai. Its slightly sweet and floral notes complement spices, giving a nice balance of flavors, and its firm, sticky texture holds up well with meats and poultry.

MAKES 4 SERVINGS

COOKING PROGRAM

• Pressure Cook •

1¼ cups	jasmine rice, rinsed	300 mL
½ tsp	salt	2 mL
1¼ cups	water	300 mL
1 tsp	vegetable oil	5 mL

TIPS

The key to perfect rice is letting the pot stand, covered, for the recommended time before releasing the pressure. Not only does this continue gently cooking the rice, but it also prevents rice and steam from clogging the steam release valve, which might happen if the pressure is released too early.

This recipe can be doubled, as long as you don't fill the pot more than halfway.

1. In the inner pot, combine rice, salt, water and oil.

2. Close and lock the lid and turn the steam release handle to Sealing. Set your Instant Pot to pressure cook on High for 1 minute.

3. When the cooking time is done, press Cancel and let stand, covered, for 10 minutes, then turn the steam release handle to venting. When the float valve drops down, remove the lid. The rice should be tender. (If more cooking time is needed, close and lock the lid and let stand for 30 seconds.)

4. Fluff rice with a fork. Serve immediately.

VARIATION

In place of the water, use ready-to-use reduced-sodium chicken broth or Low-Sodium Chicken Stock (variation, page 27) and omit the salt.

Simple Rice Pilaf

A classic rice pilaf is the perfect side dish for a variety of main dishes, especially salmon or chicken. Not only does the Instant Pot make perfect rice every time, but you can follow the variation to make a perfect one-pot meal.

MAKES 6 SERVINGS

COOKING PROGRAMS

• Sauté •
• Pressure Cook •

1 tbsp	virgin olive oil	15 mL
½	onion, finely chopped	½
1⅓ cups	long-grain white rice, rinsed	325 mL
1 cup	ready-to-use chicken broth or Chicken Stock (page 27)	250 mL
¾ cup	water	175 mL
4 tsp	chopped fresh parsley	20 mL

TIP

Short-grain white rice also works in this recipe. In step 2, increase the cooking time to 8 minutes.

1. Set your Instant Pot to sauté on Normal. When the display says Hot, add oil and heat until shimmering. Add onion and cook, stirring often, for 5 minutes or until translucent. Add rice and cook, stirring, for 1 to 2 minutes or until translucent and lightly browned. Press Cancel. Stir in broth and water.

2. Close and lock the lid and turn the steam release handle to Sealing. Set your Instant Pot to pressure cook on High for 3 minutes.

3. When the cooking time is done, press Cancel and let stand, covered, for 10 minutes, then turn the steam release handle to venting. When the float valve drops down, remove the lid. The rice should be tender. (If more cooking time is needed, close and lock the lid and let stand for 2 minutes.)

4. Fluff rice with a fork, then stir in parsley. Serve immediately.

VARIATIONS

Pot-in-Pot: To cook a complete meal, after step 1, spoon mixture into a 6-cup (1.5 L) heatproof dish. Add a recipe, such as Herbed Salmon with Asparagus (page 114), to the inner pot. Place a steam rack on top. Place a crisscross foil sling (see page 16) on the rack and place the heatproof dish in the sling. Continue with step 2.

Nutty Rice Pilaf: Add ½ diced carrot with the onion in step 1. Stir in 2½ tbsp (37 mL) slivered almonds with the parsley in step 4.

Hands-Free Risotto

Risotto is one of my go-to dishes for a simple meal or an elegant dinner. I love the taste and texture, and the way it complements so many main dishes. It can even be a tasty, filling entrée on its own if you add vegetables or seafood. If you're weary of how hands-on risotto is on the stovetop, you're going to love how easy it is in your Instant Pot — and the results are consistently fabulous!

MAKES 4 SERVINGS

COOKING PROGRAMS

• Sauté •
• Pressure Cook •

1½ tbsp	virgin olive oil	22 mL
1	onion, chopped	1
1	clove garlic, minced	1
2 cups	Arborio rice	500 mL
4 cups	ready-to-use reduced-sodium vegetable broth or Low-Sodium Vegetable Stock (variation, page 28)	1 L
1 cup	hot water (approx.)	250 mL
	Salt	
½ cup	grated Parmigiano-Reggiano cheese	125 mL
1 tbsp	butter (optional)	15 mL
	Freshly ground black pepper	

TIP

Using authentic, full-flavored Parmigiano-Reggiano creates a complex, yet subtle tango of flavors. If you can't find it, you can use regular Parmesan.

1. Set your Instant Pot to sauté on Normal. When the display says Hot, add oil and heat until shimmering. Add onion and cook, stirring, for 2 to 3 minutes or until softened. Add garlic and cook, stirring, for 30 seconds or until fragrant. Add rice, stirring to coat with oil. Press Cancel. Stir in broth, hot water and ¼ tsp (1 mL) salt.

2. Close and lock the lid and turn the steam release handle to Sealing. Set your Instant Pot to pressure cook on High for 4 minutes.

3. When the cooking time is done, press Cancel and turn the steam release handle to Venting. When the float valve drops down, remove the lid. The rice should be al dente. (If more cooking time is needed, continue pressure cooking on High for 1 minute.)

4. Set your Instant Pot to sauté on Normal. Add cheese and butter (if using); cook, stirring and adding more hot water or broth, if desired, for 1 to 3 minutes or until rice is done to your liking. Season to taste with salt and pepper. Serve immediately.

VARIATIONS

Saffron Risotto: Add a pinch of saffron with the broth in step 1.

Herbed Risotto: Add 2 tbsp (30 mL) chopped fresh thyme with the broth in step 1.

One-Pot Pasta

Making pasta in the Instant Pot is very easy if you follow these guidelines for best results. You can make pasta on its own or follow the variation to make pasta in sauce. Either way, you will find yourself using this handy method to make many a quick and easy meal.

MAKES 8 SERVINGS

COOKING PROGRAM
• Pressure Cook •

1 lb	dried pasta (see tips)	500 g
2 tsp	salt	10 mL
1 tbsp	virgin olive oil	15 mL
	Water	

1. Add pasta, salt and oil to the inner pot. Using a spoon, push pasta down evenly. Add enough water just to cover pasta, pushing pasta down as needed, then add another $1/2$ cup (125 mL) water.

2. Close and lock the lid and turn the steam release handle to Sealing. Set your Instant Pot to pressure cook on High and adjust the time to half the time recommended on the pasta package minus 1 minute. (If the cooking time is a range, use half of the higher number minus 1 minute.)

3. When the cooking time is done, press Cancel and turn the steam release handle to Venting. When the float valve drops down, remove the lid. The pasta should be al dente. (If more cooking time is needed, continue pressure cooking on High for 1 minute.) Drain off excess water, if necessary.

4. Serve immediately, add to your sauce or add to another recipe according to directions.

VARIATION

Italian-Inspired One-Pot Pasta: Increase the oil to 6 tbsp (90 mL). Skip step 1. Set your Instant Pot to sauté on Normal. When the display says Hot, add oil and heat until shimmering. Add 4 crushed garlic cloves and cook, stirring, for 1 to 2 minutes or until golden. Add a 28-oz (796 mL) can of tomatoes, lightly crushed, 1 tbsp (15 mL) finely chopped fresh basil, and salt and pepper to taste; cook, stirring, for 5 minutes. Press Cancel. Add pasta, pushing it down into sauce. Add $1\frac{1}{4}$ cups (300 mL) water to the tomato can, swishing it to collect the remaining juices, and pour on top of pasta. Continue with steps 2 and 3 (do not drain). Stir pasta and sauce. Serve warm, with grated Parmesan cheese, if desired.

TIPS

Use only dried pasta. Do not use pasta that requires less than 8 minutes cooking time. Fresh pasta usually requires 7 minutes or less to cook.

Do not use tiny pasta, such as orzo or pastina, as it may clog the steam release vent.

Do not use any pasta, such as gnocchi, that has "floating" as the doneness test, as you cannot see the pasta to tell whether it is floating.

Instant Marinara Sauce

Sometimes the simplest things are the best. Such is the case with this traditional marinara sauce made with tomatoes, garlic, hot pepper flakes and basil. Use it to complement pasta or polenta without overpowering the dish.

MAKES ABOUT 4½ CUPS (1.125 L)		

COOKING PROGRAMS		
• Sauté •		
• Pressure Cook •		

1	can (28 oz/796 mL) whole tomatoes (preferably San Marzano), with juice	1
¾ cup	water	175 mL
¼ cup	virgin olive oil	60 mL
6	cloves garlic, slivered	6
Pinch	hot pepper flakes	Pinch
	Salt	
1	sprig fresh basil	1

1. Pour tomatoes into a large bowl. Add ¾ cup (175 mL) water to the can, swishing it to collect the remaining juices. Set aside. Using your hands, crush tomatoes until pieces are about ½ inch (1 cm).

2. Set your Instant Pot to sauté on Normal. When the display says Hot, add oil and heat until shimmering. Add garlic and cook, stirring, for 1 minute or until fragrant. Add tomatoes, tomato water, hot pepper flakes and 1 tsp (5 mL) salt, stirring well. Place basil on top and just push down into sauce; do not stir. Press Cancel.

3. Close and lock the lid and turn the steam release handle to Sealing. Set your Instant Pot to pressure cook on High for 9 minutes.

4. When the cooking time is done, press Cancel and turn the steam release handle to Venting. When the float valve drops down, remove the lid. The sauce should be thickened. (If more cooking time is needed, set your Instant Pot to sauté on Less and simmer, stirring often, for 3 to 5 minutes or until thickened to your liking.) Discard basil sprig. Season to taste with salt.

TIP

Use the best canned tomatoes you can find. San Marzano tomatoes are known for their quality and rich flavor, but any high-quality brand will work.

You can use fresh, in-season tomatoes in place of canned. You will need about 10 to 12 plum (Roma) tomatoes, peeled, for this recipe. To quickly peel tomatoes, score one end of each tomato and add them to a pot of boiling water for 45 seconds or until the skin begins to wrinkle. Using tongs, quickly transfer them to a bowl of ice water, then peel and chop. Transfer tomatoes, with any accumulated juices, to a 4-cup (1 L) measuring cup and add enough water to measure $3\frac{1}{2}$ cups (875 mL). Add in place of the tomatoes and tomato water in step 2. Increase the cooking time to 11 minutes.

TIPS

The sauce can be refrigerated for up to 3 days or frozen for up to 3 months. Before freezing tomato sauce, divide it into measured amounts and label each container with the amount and date.

If you like your sauce spicier, add more hot pepper flakes in step 4, with the salt or when simmering the sauce. Pressure cooking intensifies the heat of chile peppers, so adding more than a pinch before cooking could make your sauce too spicy.

Meat Ragù

Here, a simple beef ragù gets an uptick in flavor from shredded beef chuck roast and fresh rosemary. You can make it ahead of time and use it in a variety of dishes. It works especially well on top of polenta or wide pasta noodles.

MAKES ABOUT 7 CUPS (1.75 L)

COOKING PROGRAMS
• Sauté •
• Pressure Cook •

1¾ lbs	boneless beef chuck roast, cut into 2-inch (5 cm) cubes	875 g
	Salt and freshly ground black pepper	
2 tbsp	vegetable oil (approx.)	30 mL
4	cloves garlic, minced	4
1	onion, chopped	1
2	sprigs fresh rosemary	2
1	can (28 oz/796 mL) diced tomatoes, with juice	1
1½ cups	ready-to-use reduced-sodium beef broth or Low-Sodium Beef Bone Broth (page 26)	375 mL

1. Season beef with salt and pepper. Set your Instant Pot to sauté on Normal. When the display says Hot, add 1 tbsp (15 mL) oil and heat until shimmering. Working in batches, add beef and cook, stirring, for 2 minutes or until lightly browned on all sides, adding more oil as needed between batches. Using a slotted spoon, transfer beef to a plate as it is browned. Press Cancel.

2. Set your Instant Pot to sauté on Less. Add garlic, onion and rosemary; cook, stirring, for 5 minutes or until onion is softened and lightly browned. Return beef and any accumulated juices to the pot and stir in tomatoes with juice and broth. Press Cancel.

3. Close and lock the lid and turn the steam release handle to Sealing. Set your Instant Pot to pressure cook on High for 35 minutes.

4. When the cooking time is done, press Cancel and let stand, covered, for 10 minutes, then turn the steam release handle to Venting. When the float valve drops down, remove the lid. The beef should be melt-in-your-mouth tender. (If more cooking time is needed, continue pressure cooking on High for 10 minutes, then quickly release the pressure.) Discard rosemary.

5. Using a slotted spoon, transfer beef to a large bowl. Using two forks, shred beef, discarding excess fat. Discard rosemary stems from sauce. Stir beef back into sauce.

6. Set your Instant Pot to sauté on Normal. Cook, stirring often, for 10 to 15 minutes or until sauce is thickened to your liking. Season to taste with salt and pepper.

SERVING SUGGESTION

Serve over roasted vegetables, polenta or large pasta noodles, such as pappardelle or tagliatelle.

TIP

Store sauce in smaller batches for use in multiple dishes. Divide it among airtight containers and store in the refrigerator for up to 3 days or in the freezer for up to 3 months.

All-Around Barbecue Sauce

This tasty all-around barbecue sauce is perfect for pork or chicken. Use it as is or dress it up for a specific recipe. It's sure to become your go-to barbecue sauce recipe.

MAKES ABOUT 2 CUPS (500 ML)

COOKING PROGRAM
• Pressure Cook •

1 tbsp	vegetable oil	15 mL
¾ cup	packed light brown sugar	175 mL
1 cup	apple cider vinegar	250 mL
4 tsp	smoked paprika	20 mL
2 tsp	ground cumin	10 mL
2 tsp	salt	10 mL
2 tsp	freshly ground black pepper	10 mL
1⅓ cups	ketchup	325 mL

TIPS

If using the sauce for grilling, brush it on near the end of the cooking times so it caramelizes but doesn't burn.

The cooled sauce can be refrigerated for up to 1 month or frozen for up to 6 months.

1. Add oil to the inner pot and swirl to coat the bottom. Add brown sugar and vinegar, stirring to combine. Stir in paprika, cumin, salt, pepper and ketchup.

2. Close and lock the lid and turn the steam release handle to Sealing. Set your Instant Pot to pressure cook on High for 8 minutes.

3. When the cooking time is done, press Cancel and let stand, covered, for 10 minutes, then turn the steam release handle to Venting. When the float valve drops down, remove the lid. Stir sauce, transfer to storage containers and let cool.

BREAKFASTS • BREAKFASTS • BRE
BREAKFASTS • BREAKFASTS • BR
EAKFASTS • BREAKFASTS • BRE
BREAKFASTS • BREAKFASTS • BR
EAKFASTS • BREAKFASTS • BRE
BREAKFASTS • BREAKFASTS • BR
EAKFASTS • BREAKFASTS • BRE
BREAKFASTS • BREAKFASTS • BF
EAKFASTS • BREAKFASTS • BRE
BREAKFASTS • BREAKFASTS • BF
EAKFASTS • BREAKFASTS • BRE
BREAKFASTS • BREAKFASTS • BF
EAKFASTS • BREAKFASTS • BRE
BREAKFASTS • BREAKFASTS • BF
EAKFASTS • BREAKFASTS • BRE
BREAKFASTS • BREAKFASTS • BF
EAKFASTS • BREAKFASTS • BRE

BREAKFASTS

Classic Old-Fashioned Oatmeal

If you want a nice, warm, filling bowl of oatmeal to jump-start your day, using the Instant Pot is an easy, hands-off way to make it. While it doesn't save cooking time, it does save you from puttering around with it. You can make it just for yourself, or for up to four people.

MAKES 1 SERVING

COOKING PROGRAM
• Pressure Cook •

- **2-cup (500 mL) heatproof bowl**
- **Steam rack**

⅓ cup	large-flake (old-fashioned) rolled oats	75 mL
Pinch	salt	Pinch
⅔ cup	water or milk	150 mL
½ tsp	butter (optional)	2 mL

TIPS

Start step 1 about 30 minutes before you are ready to eat. This will allow enough time for the cooker to come up to pressure, cook the oatmeal and then release the pressure.

You can double or quadruple this recipe. Increase the size of the heatproof bowl to one that holds twice the volume of your ingredients, so that it is only halfway full. If necessary, use a crisscross foil sling (see page 16) to help you lift the bowl out of the pot. Divide oatmeal among serving bowls.

In place of water or milk, you can use soy milk, rice milk or nut milk. If using coconut milk, replace only ⅓ cup (75 mL) of the water with coconut milk.

1. In the heatproof bowl, combine oats, salt, water and butter (if using).
2. Add 2 cups (500 mL) hot water to the inner pot and place the steam rack in the pot. Place the bowl on the rack.
3. Close and lock the lid and turn the steam release handle to Sealing. Set your Instant Pot to pressure cook on High for 7 minutes.
4. When the cooking time is done, press Cancel and let stand, covered, until the float valve drops down, then remove the lid. The oatmeal should be creamy. (If more cooking time is needed, continue pressure cooking on High for 1 minute, then quickly release the pressure.)
5. Using the handles of the rack, carefully remove the rack and bowl. Stir oats and serve immediately.

SERVING SUGGESTION

Serve sprinkled with ground cinnamon or granulated or brown sugar, or drizzled with pure maple syrup or honey.

VARIATIONS

Quick-Cooking Oats: Replace the large-flake rolled oats with quick-cooking rolled oats. In step 3, decrease the cooking time to 1 minute.

Creamy Oatmeal: Decrease the oats to ¼ cup (60 mL) and increase the water or milk to ¾ cup (175 mL).

Peanut Butter Banana Oatmeal

This creamy oatmeal breakfast with its crowd-pleasing flavors of peanut butter and banana is a great way to start your day. Power up with this nourishing breakfast bowl, and you will feel like you can tackle anything.

MAKES 2 SERVINGS

COOKING PROGRAM
• Pressure Cook •

- **4-cup (1 L) heatproof bowl**
- **Steam rack**

⅔ cup	large-flake (old-fashioned) rolled oats	150 mL
½ cup	banana slices (about ½ banana)	125 mL
⅛ tsp	salt	0.5 mL
1⅓ cups	milk	325 mL
2 tbsp	peanut butter (approx.)	30 mL
1 tsp	packed brown sugar (optional)	5 mL

> **TIP**
> You can use frozen sliced bananas in place of fresh, if desired.

1. In the heatproof bowl, combine oats, banana slices, salt and milk.

2. Add 2 cups (500 mL) hot water to the inner pot and place the steam rack in the pot. Place a crisscross foil sling (see page 16) on the rack and place the bowl in the sling.

3. Close and lock the lid and turn the steam release handle to Sealing. Set your Instant Pot to pressure cook on High for 7 minutes.

4. When the cooking time is done, press Cancel and let stand, covered, until the float valve drops down, then remove the lid. The oatmeal should be creamy. (If more cooking time is needed, continue pressure cooking on High for 1 minute, then quickly release the pressure.)

5. Using the foil sling, remove bowl from the pot and immediately stir in peanut butter until well incorporated. Taste and add more peanut butter, if desired.

6. Divide oatmeal between serving bowls and sprinkle with brown sugar, if desired.

VARIATION

Substitute an equal amount of any dried or frozen fruits or berries for the bananas and, if desired, omit the peanut butter. If the fruit has been preserved with sugar, adjust the amount of sugar added in step 6 to taste.

Hearty Steel-Cut Oats

Breakfast is such an important way to start the day. With a hearty bowl of steel-cut oats, you'll feel like you are ready to tackle anything. Make it to serve five people today, or make it ahead to enjoy 5 days of ready-in-minutes breakfasts.

MAKES 5 SERVINGS

COOKING PROGRAMS

• Sauté •
• Pressure Cook •

• **Five 1-pint (500 mL) canning jars with lids (optional)**

1 tbsp	butter or vegetable oil	15 mL
1¼ cups	steel-cut oats	300 mL
1 tsp	salt	5 mL
3½ cups	water or milk	875 mL

TIPS

You can make smaller amounts of this recipe. Use ¼ cup (60 mL) oats and ¾ cup (175 mL) liquid per serving.

If you prefer not to reheat oatmeal in the microwave, you can do so in your Instant Pot. Spoon oatmeal into the inner pot. Set your Instant Pot to sauté on More and cook, stirring often, for 5 minutes or until oatmeal is warmed through.

1. Set your Instant Pot to sauté on Normal. When the display says Hot, add butter and heat until melted. Add oats and cook, stirring, for 2 to 3 minutes or until lightly toasted and fragrant. Press Cancel. Stir in salt and water.

2. Close and lock the lid and turn the steam release handle to Sealing. Set your Instant Pot to pressure cook on High for 12 minutes.

3. When the cooking time is done, press Cancel and let stand, covered, until the float valve drops down, then remove the lid. The oatmeal should be creamy. (If more cooking time is needed, continue cooking on High for 2 minutes, then quickly release the pressure.) Stir oats. Serve immediately or continue with step 4 to store.

4. Let oatmeal stand for at least 10 minutes or until cooled to room temperature. Spoon oatmeal into jars. Screw lids on and refrigerate jars up to 5 days.

5. To reheat, uncover jar(s) and stir oatmeal. Microwave jar(s) on High for 2 to 3 minutes or until hot.

Butternut Squash and Steel-Cut Oats

The inviting flavors of fall coalesce in a hearty bowl of steel-cut oatmeal. Keep the ingredients on hand so you can make it whenever you wish. When you feel like mixing it up, try one of the variations.

MAKES 4 SERVINGS

COOKING PROGRAMS

• Sauté •
• Pressure Cook •

1 tbsp	butter or vegetable oil	15 mL
1 cup	steel-cut oats	250 mL
1½ cups	frozen butternut squash cubes	375 mL
¼ tsp	salt	1 mL
3 cups	water	750 mL
	Pure maple syrup (optional)	

TIP

When preparing oats under pressure, make sure to fill the pot no more than halfway. If the cooker is more than halfway full, the pressure release device may become clogged as the porridge froths up under pressure.

1. Set your Instant Pot to sauté on Normal. When the display says Hot, add butter and heat until melted. Add oats and cook, stirring, for 2 to 3 minutes or until lightly toasted and fragrant. Press Cancel. Add squash, salt and water, stirring well.

2. Close and lock the lid and turn the steam release handle to Sealing. Set your Instant Pot to pressure cook on High for 12 minutes.

3. When the cooking time is done, press Cancel and let stand, covered, until the float valve drops down, then remove the lid. The oats should be done to your liking. (If more cooking time is needed, continue pressure cooking on High for 5 minutes, then quickly release the pressure.) Stir oats. Stir in maple syrup to taste, if desired. Serve immediately.

VARIATION

Pumpkin and Cinnamon Oatmeal: Replace the squash with ¾ cup (175 mL) pumpkin purée (not pie filling) and stir in ¼ tsp (1 mL) ground cinnamon. Serve sprinkled with more cinnamon, if desired.

Perfectly Cooked Eggs

Pressure cooking is an ideal way to cook eggs because you don't have to use older eggs to make them easier to peel — the shell almost slides right off — and they are done to perfection. You can soft-cook, medium-cook, hard-cook or even poach the eggs, as you like them.

MAKES 1 TO 6 EGGS

COOKING PROGRAM

• Pressure Cook •

• **Steam rack**

| 1 to 6 | large eggs, in the shell | 1 to 6 |

1. Add 1 cup (250 mL) hot water to the inner pot and place the steam rack in the pot. Place egg(s) on the rack.

2. Close and lock the lid and turn the steam release handle to Sealing. Set your Instant Pot to pressure cook on Low for 3 minutes for soft-cooked or 5 minutes for medium-cooked (see also variations).

3. When the cooking time is done, press Cancel and turn the steam release handle to Venting. When the float valve drops down, remove the lid. Carefully peel egg under cold running water and transfer to a plate. Alternatively, transfer each egg to an egg cup. Using a spoon, tap around the top portion of the egg (about one-third from the top) and remove the shell.

VARIATIONS

Hard-Cooked Eggs: Use as many eggs as will fit in your pot by stacking. Pressure cook on Low for 6 minutes. When the cooking time is up, press Cancel and let stand, covered, until the float valve drops down, then remove the lid. If eating warm, peel them as soon as you can handle them and transfer each egg to a plate or an egg cup. If using cold, transfer eggs to a bowl of cold water; when cold, crack and discard shell.

Poached Eggs: Spray one to six 4-oz (125 mL) ramekin(s) with nonstick cooking spray. Crack an egg into each prepared ramekin, centering yolk as much as possible. Cover ramekin tightly with foil and place on rack, stacking ramekins as necessary, like stacking bricks. Pressure cook on Low for 3 minutes. When the cooking time is up, quickly release the pressure. Remove ramekin from pot and uncover. Serve egg in ramekin or slide out onto an English muffin, toast or a serving plate.

TIPS

Do not poke holes in eggs before pressure cooking.

You can use hard-cooked eggs (see variation) to make snacks, salads and deviled eggs.

Egg-Stuffed Bell Pepper Boats

Baked eggs floating in a steamed bell pepper cup, sprinkled with a bit of Parmesan and basil, makes for a delightful breakfast, perfect for vegetarians and meat lovers alike.

MAKES 2 SERVINGS

COOKING PROGRAM

• Pressure Cook •

• **Steam rack**

1	medium bell pepper (any color)	1
2	large eggs	2
	Salt and freshly ground black pepper	
	Grated Parmesan cheese	
	Chopped fresh basil	

TIPS

Choose bell peppers that are long and narrow. If the halved peppers are deeper than 2 inches (5 cm), cut the edges of the peppers to that height.

Using silicone-coated tongs to remove the peppers from the pressure cooker will help you avoid poking through the skin of the peppers. If you don't have them, just use regular tongs.

1. Cut bell pepper in half lengthwise and remove the stem, seeds and white ribs.

2. Crack an egg into each pepper half. Season with salt and pepper. For a medium-soft yolk, cover top of pepper loosely with foil. For a firm yolk, do not cover.

3. Add 1 cup (250 mL) hot water to the inner pot and place the steam rack in the pot. Arrange pepper halves on the rack.

4. Close and lock the lid and turn the steam release handle to Sealing. Set your Instant Pot to pressure cook on Low for 4 minutes.

5. When the cooking time is done, press Cancel and turn the steam release handle to Venting. When the float valve drops down, remove the lid. The egg whites should be opaque. (If more cooking time is needed or the yolk is not done to your liking, continue pressure cooking on Low for 1 minute.)

6. Using silicone-coated tongs, carefully transfer pepper boats to serving plates. Serve sprinkled with cheese and garnished with basil.

VARIATION

Italian Breakfast Boats: Before adding the egg in step 2, add 1 tbsp (15 mL) cooked chopped pancetta to the bottom of each pepper. Sprinkle each with 1 tbsp (15 mL) shredded mozzarella cheese before adding the egg. Omit the Parmesan, if desired.

Roasted Red Pepper and Cheddar Casserole

A scrumptious vegetarian casserole is a satisfying way to start your day. The combination of peppers, cheese and eggs makes this breakfast dish warm and inviting.

MAKES 4 SERVINGS

COOKING PROGRAM

• Pressure Cook •

- **6-cup (1.5 L) round soufflé dish, bottom and sides buttered**
- **Steam rack**

6	slices day-old bread, cubed (about 5 cups/1.25 L)	6
2	roasted red peppers, drained and finely chopped	2
1 cup	shredded sharp (old) Cheddar cheese	250 mL
3	large eggs	3
½ tsp	salt	2 mL
¼ tsp	freshly ground black pepper	1 mL
1 cup	milk	250 mL

1. Layer half the bread cubes in prepared soufflé dish. Sprinkle evenly with roasted peppers and cheese. Layer the remaining bread cubes on top.

2. In a small bowl, whisk eggs. Whisk in salt, pepper and milk. Pour over bread cubes, gently pressing down on bread to cover with liquid.

3. Add 1 cup (250 mL) hot water to the inner pot and place the steam rack in the pot. Place a crisscross foil sling (see page 16) on the rack and place the soufflé dish in the sling.

4. Close and lock the lid and turn the steam release handle to Sealing. Set your Instant Pot to pressure cook on High for 10 minutes.

5. When the cooking time is done, press Cancel and turn the steam release handle to Venting. When the float valve drops down, remove the lid. A knife inserted in the center should come out clean. (If more cooking time is needed, continue pressure cooking on High for 2 minutes.)

6. Using the foil sling, remove dish from the pot. Cut into 4 wedges and serve immediately.

TIPS

Hearty breads, such as country-style, sourdough or French, work best in this recipe because they retain their shape better.

If you like a golden brown top, after step 5, preheat broiler, with the top rack about 5 inches (12.5 cm) from the heat source. Carefully transfer casserole to oven and broil for 5 minutes or until top is golden brown. Let stand for 5 minutes, then cut into 4 wedges and serve immediately.

Streusel Coffee Cake (page 52)

Fireside Tomato Soup (page 65)

Southwestern Pulled Pork Chili (page 71)

Coconut Curry Beef (page 78) and
Foolproof Jasmine Rice (page 32)

Pepperoncini Beef Roast (page 79)

Creamy Beef Stroganoff (page 80)

Maple Dijon Pork Medallions (page 86) and
Buttery Garlic Mashed Potatoes (page 155)

Almost Rotisserie Chicken (page 98) and
Sweet and Easy Corn on the Cob (page 151)

Easy Blueberry French Toast Pudding

Who can deny the sweet delight of French toast? Cinnamon swirl bread is the magic ingredient, along with blueberries and pure maple syrup. The best part is, you can eat it for breakfast or serve it up as bread pudding for dessert.

MAKES 4 SERVINGS

COOKING PROGRAM

• Pressure Cook •

- **4-cup (1 L) round soufflé dish, bottom and sides buttered**
- **Steam rack**

3	large eggs	3
¼ tsp	salt	1 mL
1½ cups	milk	375 mL
3 tbsp	pure maple syrup	45 mL
1 lb	cinnamon swirl bread, crusts trimmed off and bread cubed	500 g
½ cup	dried blueberries	125 mL

1. In a large bowl, whisk eggs. Stir in salt, milk and maple syrup. Fold in bread cubes and blueberries, gently pressing down on bread to cover with liquid. Let stand for 30 minutes or until bread has absorbed liquid.

2. Pour bread mixture into prepared soufflé dish. Add 1 cup (250 mL) hot water to the inner pot and place the steam rack in the pot. Place the soufflé dish on the rack and cover with foil.

3. Close and lock the lid and turn the steam release handle to Sealing. Set your Instant Pot to pressure cook on High for 30 minutes.

4. When the cooking time is done, press Cancel and turn the steam release handle to Venting. When the float valve drops down, remove the lid. A tester inserted in the center should come out clean. (If more cooking time is needed, continue pressure cooking on High for 5 minutes.)

5. Using the handles of the rack, carefully remove the rack and dish from the pot. Remove foil and let stand for 5 minutes. Cut into 4 wedges and serve immediately.

SERVING SUGGESTION

If serving this dish for dessert, add a scoop of ice cream or a dollop of whipped cream on top.

VARIATION

Try a cinnamon swirl bread made with raisins, apples or chocolate chips. You can keep or omit the dried blueberries when using one of these breads.

TIPS

This recipe serves 6 people as a dessert.

If you prefer to keep the crust on the bread, use 12 oz (375 g) bread, cubed.

Ham and Cheddar Egg Bites

We all know that breakfast is the most important meal of the day. And when you can make tasty, nourishing egg bites in a jiffy in your Instant Pot, there's no need to skip it or grab fast food. You can even take these with you and hustle out the door.

MAKES 6 OR 7 EGG BITES

COOKING PROGRAM

• Pressure Cook •

- **Blender**
- **Round silicone egg bites mold (see tip) with 6 or 7 cups, sprayed with nonstick cooking spray**
- **Steam rack**

4	large eggs	4
1½ cups	shredded Cheddar cheese, divided	375 mL
½ cup	cottage cheese	125 mL
¼ cup	heavy or whipping (35%) cream	60 mL
2 tsp	dried onion flakes	10 mL
Pinch	salt	Pinch
¼ cup	finely chopped cooked ham	60 mL

1. In blender, combine eggs, 1 cup (250 mL) Cheddar cheese, cottage cheese, cream, onion flakes and salt; purée until fairly smooth. Stir in ham and the remaining Cheddar cheese.

2. Pour into prepared egg bites mold, dividing evenly between cups. Place mold cover loosely on top.

3. Add 1 cup (250 mL) hot water to the inner pot and place the steam rack in the pot. Place the egg bites mold on the rack.

4. Close and lock the lid and turn the steam release handle to Sealing. Set your Instant Pot to pressure cook on High for 8 minutes.

5. When the cooking time is done, press Cancel and let stand, covered, for 5 minutes, then turn the steam release handle to Venting. When the float valve drops down, remove the lid. A tester inserted in the center should come out clean. (If more cooking time is needed, continue pressure cooking on High for 1 minute.)

6. To serve immediately, invert a plate on top of the mold, flip it over and gently squeeze the cups to release the egg bites. To store, let cool, then cover mold and refrigerate for up to 5 days; pop egg bites out of the mold as you need them.

VARIATION

Use 4 slices of chopped cooked bacon in place of the ham.

SERVING SUGGESTION

Add one of these to the center of a toasted English muffin for a grab-and-go breakfast sandwich.

TIPS

Round silicone egg bites molds can be found online with other popular Instant Pot accessories. You can also use one-piece silicone molds that are used to store individual servings of baby food.

Reheat individual egg bites in the microwave on High for 10 seconds.

Fiery Jumbo Cornbread Muffins

For those who like a little bit of fire in their belly to start the day, these jalapeño popper muffins are just the thing. This recipe makes enough for four people, or you can store them all for yourself! They also make a wonderful accompaniment to chilis and stews.

MAKES 4 MUFFINS

COOKING PROGRAM

• Pressure Cook •

- **4 jumbo silicone baking cups or 4-oz (125 mL) ramekins, buttered**
- **Steam rack**

1	package (8½ oz/240 g) corn muffin mix (such as Jiffy)	1
3 tbsp	shredded Monterey Jack cheese	45 mL
1	large egg	1
½ cup	milk or buttermilk	125 mL
2 tbsp	butter, melted	30 mL
1½ tbsp	chopped drained pickled jalapeños	22 mL

1. In a medium bowl, combine muffin mix, cheese, egg, milk, butter and jalapeños, mixing well. The batter will be coarse. Let rest for 3 to 4 minutes, then stir. Spoon batter into baking cups, dividing evenly.

2. Add 1 cup (250 mL) hot water to the inner pot and place the steam rack in the pot. Arrange baking cups on the rack.

3. Close and lock the lid and turn the steam release handle to Sealing. Set your Instant Pot to pressure cook on High for 20 minutes.

4. When the cooking time is done, press Cancel and let stand, covered, for 10 minutes, then turn the steam release handle to Venting. When the float valve drops down, remove the lid. A tester inserted in the center of a muffin should come out clean. (If more cooking time is needed, continue pressure cooking on High for 3 minutes, then quickly release the pressure.) Using silicone oven mitts, carefully lift rack with muffins out of the pot and let muffins cool to room temperature on rack.

SERVING SUGGESTIONS

Serve spread with jam or preserves for breakfast.

Serve with a bowl of chili for lunch or dinner.

TIPS

For a milder chile flavor, substitute chopped canned green chiles for the jalapeños and sharp (old) Cheddar cheese for the Monterey Jack.

The muffins can be stored in an airtight container at room temperature for up to 3 days.

Streusel Coffee Cake

Oh yeah, baby, now we're talking! Not only is pressure-cooked coffee cake quick and easy, but you no longer have to heat up your oven on a hot summer day.

MAKES 6 SERVINGS

COOKING PROGRAM

• Pressure Cook •

- **7-inch (18 cm) nonstick fluted tube pan (such as a Bundt or kugelhopf), greased**
- **Steam rack**

2⅓ cups	all-purpose baking mix (such as Bisquick), divided	575 mL
½ cup	packed brown sugar, divided	125 mL
½ tsp	ground cinnamon	2 mL
4 tbsp	cold butter, divided	60 mL
1	large egg	1
⅔ cup	water	150 mL

1. In a small bowl, combine ⅓ cup (75 mL) baking mix, ⅓ cup (175 mL) brown sugar and cinnamon. Using a pastry blender or two knives, cut in 2 tbsp (30 mL) butter until crumbly. Sprinkle half the streusel mixture in bottom of prepared pan.

2. In a medium bowl, combine the remaining baking mix and brown sugar. Cut in the remaining butter until crumbly.

3. In a measuring cup or bowl, whisk egg and water. Add to dry ingredients and stir until just combined.

4. Pour half the batter over streusel mixture in pan. Sprinkle with the remaining streusel. Top with the remaining batter.

5. Add 1 cup (250 mL) hot water to the inner pot and place the steam rack in the pot. Place the pan on the rack.

6. Close and lock the lid and turn the steam release handle to Sealing. Set your Instant Pot to pressure cook on High for 25 minutes.

7. When the cooking time is done, press Cancel and let stand, covered, for 10 minutes, then turn the steam release handle to Venting. When the float valve drops down, remove the lid. A tester inserted in the center should come out clean. (If more cooking time is needed, continue pressure cooking on High for 3 minutes, then quickly release the pressure.)

8. Using the handles of the rack, carefully remove the rack and pan. Let cake cool to room temperature in pan on rack, then invert onto a plate and cut into slices.

TIPS

For a richer coffee cake, use milk in place of water.

Remove the lid carefully to prevent any moisture on the lid from dripping onto the cake.

In place of the Bundt or Kugelhopf pan, use a 7-inch (18 cm) springform tube pan and sprinkle all of the streusel in the bottom of the prepared pan before adding the batter.

Homemade Yogurt

Yogurt is so easy to make in your Instant Pot, but you will need to allow at least 16 hours to pasteurize and incubate the milk and then cool the yogurt until it is ready to use. Yogurt-making takes practice to get exactly the flavors and consistency you prefer, but it is so worth the effort.

MAKES ABOUT 4 CUPS (1 L)

COOKING PROGRAMS
- Pressure Cook •
- Yogurt •

- **5 sterilized canning jars (preferably 8 oz/250 mL), with two-piece lids or screw caps**
- **Steam rack**
- **Instant-read thermometer**

4 cups	whole milk	1 L
	Greek yogurt with live active cultures (see tips)	

Jar Method

1. Divide milk evenly among jars, leaving room at the top for the yogurt and leaving jars uncovered. Add 1½ cups (375 mL) hot water to the inner pot and place the steam rack in the pot. Place the jars on the rack. Close and lock the lid and turn the steam release handle to Sealing. Set your Instant Pot to pressure cook on High for 0 minutes.

2. Meanwhile, add 2 tbsp (30 mL) yogurt to a measuring cup with a pour spout.

3. When the cooking time is done, press Cancel and let stand, covered, until the float valve drops down, then remove the lid. An instant-read thermometer inserted into the milk in each jar should register at least 180°F (82°C). (If more cooking time is needed, continue pressure cooking on High for 0 minutes.)

4. Carefully transfer jars to a wire rack and let cool until an instant-read thermometer inserted in the center of a jar registers between 110°F and 115°F (43°C and 46°C). Remove and discard any skin on the milk.

5. Spoon 1 tbsp (15 mL) milk from each jar into the yogurt, stirring well. Pour back into the jars, dividing evenly.

6. Return the uncovered jars to the rack. Close and lock the lid and turn the steam release handle to Venting or Sealing. Select Yogurt and set your Instant Pot to cook on Normal for 6 to 12 hours (see tip).

7. When the incubation time is done, press Cancel and remove the lid.

8. Remove jars from the pot, cover with flat lids and twist on screwbands until there is a little resistance. Refrigerate for at least 6 hours, until chilled, or for up to 10 days.

Pot Method

1. Add milk to the inner pot. Close and lock the lid and turn the steam release handle to Venting or Sealing. Select Yogurt and adjust the temperature to More. The display will say Boil.

2. Meanwhile, add 2 tbsp (30 mL) yogurt to a measuring cup with a pour spout.

3. When the display says Yogt, press Cancel and remove the lid. Using a rubber spatula, stir milk, without scraping the bottom. An instant-read thermometer inserted into the milk in several places should register at least 180°F (82°C). (If more cooking time is needed, set your Instant Pot to slow cook on Less for 5 minutes.)

4. Transfer pot to a wire rack and let cool, uncovered, until an instant-read thermometer registers between 110°F and 115°F (43°C and 46°C). Remove and discard any skin on the milk.

5. Spoon ¼ cup (60 mL) milk from the pot into the yogurt, stirring well. Pour back into the pot.

6. Return the inner pot to the Instant Pot. Close and lock the lid and turn the steam release handle to Venting or Sealing. Select Yogurt and set your Instant Pot to cook on Normal for 6 to 12 hours (see tip).

7. When the incubation time is done, press Cancel and remove the lid.

8. Spoon yogurt into jars, cover with flat lids and twist on screwbands until there is a little resistance. Refrigerate for at least 6 hours, until chilled, or for up to 10 days.

VARIATIONS

Homemade Greek Yogurt: After step 7, pour the yogurt into a nut milk bag or fine-mesh kitchen towel set in a strainer over a bowl. Let drain in the refrigerator for 2 to 6 hours or until desired consistency. (The liquid left in the bowl is whey. Whey can be refrigerated for up to 7 days for use in smoothies and juices, to add protein, vitamins and minerals. Whey can also be used as a cooking liquid for rice, grains and pasta.) Spoon yogurt into jars, cover with flat lids and twist on screwbands until there is a little resistance.

Flavored Yogurt: After the yogurt has chilled, add vanilla extract and either liquid honey or pure maple syrup, starting with a small amount and adding more to taste; stir well.

Jam or Jelly Yogurt: After the yogurt has chilled, add jam or jelly, starting with a small amount and adding more to taste; stir well.

Berry Yogurt: After the yogurt has chilled, add fresh or thawed frozen berries, starting with a small amount and adding more to taste; stir well.

TIPS

Purchase high-quality yogurt with live active cultures to use as your starter. Choose a plain yogurt that you know you like.

Save some of your homemade yogurt, in a separate jar, to use as the starter for your next batch. Homemade yogurt can be refrigerated for up to 7 days for use as an active starter.

You can use fewer larger canning jars, as long as they fit in the inner pot on top of the steam rack.

Use only jars and lids or screw caps that are specifically made for canning; they will reduce the potential for breakage and will properly store your yogurt.

Before starting, make sure all of your containers and tools are sanitized.

Adjust the yogurt incubation time in step 6 according to your taste preferences. Longer incubation times will yield a tangier yogurt. Taste-test the yogurt after 6 hours, then every hour until it is done to your liking. Do not reduce the time to less than 6 hours, as the yogurt will not set properly in less time.

During the yogurt-making process, it is very important to place your Instant Pot where it will not be bumped or moved, to ensure that the yogurt sets properly.

SOUPS, STEWS AND CHILIS • SOUPS, STEWS AND CHILIS • SOUPS, STEWS AND CHILIS • SOUPS, STEWS AND CHILIS • SOUPS, STEWS AND CHILIS • SOUPS, STEWS AND CHILIS • SOUPS, STEWS AND CHILIS • SOUPS, STEWS AND CHILIS • SOUPS, STEWS AND CHILIS • SOUPS, STEWS AND CHILIS • SOUPS, STEWS AND CHILIS • SOUPS, STEWS AND CHILIS • SOUPS, STEWS AND CHILIS • SOUPS, STEWS AND CHILIS • SOUPS, STEWS AND CHILIS • SOUPS, STEWS AND CHILIS •

SOUPS, STEWS AND CHILIS

Bacon and Corn Chowder

This soup could easily be described as "comfort in a bowl." It starts off with smoky, salty bacon, then adds a rich layer of sweet, tender corn. Finally, that scrumptious combo is swirled in a rich, creamy sauce.

MAKES 6 SERVINGS

COOKING PROGRAMS

• Sauté •
• Pressure Cook •

4 oz	bacon, chopped	125 g
½ cup	chopped onion	125 mL
2	potatoes, peeled (if desired) and diced	2
3 cups	ready-to-use chicken broth or Chicken Stock (page 27)	750 mL
1 lb	frozen sweet corn kernels (preferably bicolor)	500 g
1½ cups	half-and-half (10%) cream	375 mL
	Salt and freshly ground black pepper	

1. Set your Instant Pot to sauté on Normal. Add bacon and cook, stirring occasionally, for 5 to 7 minutes or until just crisp. Using a slotted spoon, transfer bacon to a plate lined with a paper towel and let cool.

2. Add onion to the bacon fat in the pot and cook, stirring often, for 5 minutes or until softened. Stir in potatoes and broth, scraping up any browned bits from the bottom of the pot. Stir in corn. Press Cancel.

3. Close and lock the lid and turn the steam release handle to Sealing. Set your Instant Pot to pressure cook on High for 4 minutes.

4. When the cooking time is done, press Cancel and turn the steam release handle to Venting. When the float valve drops down, remove the lid. The potatoes and corn should be tender. (If more cooking time is needed, continue pressure cooking on High for 1 minute.)

5. Set your Instant Pot to sauté on Less. Stir in cream and three-quarters of the bacon; cook, stirring, for 2 to 3 minutes or until steaming. Season to taste with salt and pepper. Serve garnished with the remaining bacon.

VARIATIONS

Substitute ½ cup (125 mL) Holy Trinity flavor base (page 19) for the chopped onions.

For a creamier chowder, after step 4, stir half the corn kernels into the soup. Using an immersion blender, blend soup until creamy. Continue with step 5. Add the remaining corn with the bacon.

Moroccan-Inspired Lentil Soup

The warm and spicy notes of Moroccan cuisine are married with vegetables and nutrient-packed lentils in a creamy, mouthwatering soup. Perfect for cold and frosty days, this soup will please vegetarians and meat lovers alike.

MAKES 6 SERVINGS

COOKING PROGRAMS

• Sauté •
• Pressure Cook •

- **Immersion blender (see tip, page 63)**

2 tbsp	vegetable oil	30 mL
1	large onion, chopped	1
1½ tbsp	ras el hanout (see tips)	22 mL
2	large carrots, chopped	2
1½ cups	dried red lentils, rinsed	375 mL
	Salt	
4 cups	ready-to-use reduced-sodium vegetable or chicken broth, Low-Sodium Vegetable Stock (variation, page 28) or Low-Sodium Chicken Stock (variation, page 27)	1 L
	Freshly ground black pepper	

1. Set your Instant Pot to sauté on Normal. When the display says Hot, add oil and heat until shimmering. Add onion and cook, stirring often, for 5 minutes or until softened. Stir in ras el hanout and cook, stirring, for 30 seconds. Stir in carrots, lentils, ½ tsp (2 mL) salt and broth. Press Cancel.

2. Close and lock the lid and turn the steam release handle to Sealing. Set your Instant Pot to pressure cook on High for 10 minutes.

3. When the cooking time is done, press Cancel and turn the steam release handle to Venting. When the float valve drops down, remove the lid. The lentils and carrots should be tender. (If more cooking time is needed, continue pressure cooking on High for 1 minute.)

4. Using the immersion blender, purée soup until smooth. Season to taste with salt and pepper.

TIPS

Ras el hanout is a traditional Moroccan spice blend that combines many different spices. It can be found in the spice section of the grocery store. You can use it on a variety of dishes made with poultry, pork, beef of lamb. It works especially well when combined with honey.

Use a ras el hanout blend without added salt.

If you can't find ras el hanout, you can make your own. In a small bowl, combine the following ground spices: 1 tsp (5 mL) each cumin, ginger and turmeric, ¾ tsp (3 mL) cinnamon, ½ tsp (2 mL) each allspice, black pepper, cardamom, coriander, nutmeg and paprika, and ¼ tsp (1 mL) cayenne pepper. Makes about 3 tbsp (45 mL).

Do not use green or brown lentils, as the results will not be the same.

Senate Bean Soup

This renowned soup has been served in the U.S. Senate since the early 1900s. Its simplicity and depth of flavor are two of the many reasons it has survived the test of time.

MAKES 6 SERVINGS

COOKING PROGRAMS
• Sauté •
• Pressure Cook •

2½ cups	dried navy (white pea) beans (about 1 lb/500 g)	625 mL
	Water	
3 tbsp	butter	45 mL
1	large onion, finely chopped (about 1½ cups/375 mL)	1
2	cloves garlic, chopped	2
2 cups	diced cooked ham	500 mL
	Salt and freshly ground black pepper	
	Minced fresh parsley	

1. Place beans in a large bowl, add 12 cups (3 L) cold water and let soak at room temperature for 8 hours or overnight. Drain and rinse beans.

2. Set your Instant Pot to sauté on Normal. When the display says Hot, add butter and heat until melted. Add onion and cook, stirring often, for 7 minutes or until lightly browned. Add garlic and cook, stirring, for 1 minute or until fragrant. Stir in beans, ham, ½ tsp (2 mL) salt and 5 cups (1.25 L) water, stirring well. Press Cancel.

3. Close and lock the lid and turn the steam release handle to Sealing. Set your Instant Pot to pressure cook on High for 7 minutes.

4. When the cooking time is done, press Cancel and let stand, covered, until the float valve drops down. Remove the lid. The beans should be tender. (If more cooking time is needed, continue pressure cooking on High for 1 minute, then quickly release the pressure.) Skim off and discard fat.

5. Using a potato masher, mash some of the beans until the soup is your desired consistency. Season to taste with salt and pepper. Serve immediately, garnished with parsley.

TIPS

When preparing legumes of any type, make sure to fill the pot no more than halfway. Do not attempt to double or triple the recipe unless you are using a large-capacity cooker; otherwise, the exhaust valve may become clogged as the beans froth up under pressure.

Beans can be presoaked, drained and frozen up to 3 months in advance. If you are using your beans for various recipes, measure the dry and soaked weights of the beans and mark them on the container before freezing.

The soup can be stored in airtight containers in the refrigerator for up to 3 days or in the freezer for up to 3 months. Thaw in the refrigerator or defrost in the microwave. Reheat in a saucepan over medium heat, stirring occasionally, until warmed through.

Hearty Black Bean Soup

This easy-to-make soup will surprise you with its complex flavors and delightful textures. Simply by changing the heat level of the salsa to suit your taste, you can make the soup mellow or fire-burning.

MAKES 6 SERVINGS

COOKING PROGRAMS

• Sauté •
• Pressure Cook •

2 cups	dried black beans	500 mL
	Water	
1 tbsp	vegetable oil	15 mL
2	cloves garlic, minced	2
2	bay leaves	2
2½ cups	chunky salsa	625 mL
	Salt and freshly ground black pepper	
2 tbsp	freshly squeezed lime juice	30 mL
	Chopped fresh cilantro (optional)	

TIPS

This recipe is meant for Instant Pots that are 6 quarts (6 L) or larger. If you are using a smaller cooker, cut the recipe in half. Do not fill the pot more than halfway.

The soup can be stored in airtight containers in the refrigerator for up to 3 days or in the freezer for up to 3 months. Thaw in the refrigerator or defrost in the microwave. Reheat in a saucepan over medium heat, stirring occasionally, until warmed through.

For freezer storage, measure soup into serving-size portions and label the containers.

1. Place beans in a large bowl, add 8 cups (2 L) cold water and let soak at room temperature for 8 hours or overnight. Drain and rinse beans.

2. Set your Instant Pot to sauté on Normal. When the display says Hot, add oil and heat until shimmering. Add garlic and cook, stirring, for 1 minute or until fragrant. Stir in beans, bay leaves, 6 cups (1.5 L) water and salsa. Press Cancel.

3. Close and lock the lid and turn the steam release handle to Sealing. Set your Instant Pot to pressure cook on High for 8 minutes.

4. When the cooking time is done, press Cancel and let stand, covered, for 15 minutes, then turn the steam release handle to Venting. When the float valve drops down, remove the lid. The beans should be tender. (If more cooking time is needed, continue pressure cooking on High for 1 minute, then quickly release the pressure.) Discard bay leaves. Season to taste with salt and pepper. Stir in lime juice. Serve garnished with cilantro, if using.

SERVING SUGGESTION

Serve with cornbread, for a delightful balance of flavors.

Beer Cheese Soup

Stop at almost any restaurant or tavern in the state of Wisconsin and you are bound to find this traditional soup on the menu. And for good reason: beer and cheese are two of the state's hallmarks, and this creamy, rich soup will melt your heart.

MAKES 6 SERVINGS

COOKING PROGRAMS
• Sauté •
• Pressure Cook or Slow Cook •

• **Immersion blender (see tip)**

3 tbsp	butter	45 mL
2	onions, finely chopped	2
¼ cup	all-purpose flour, divided	60 mL
	Freshly ground black pepper	
4 cups	ready-to-use reduced-sodium chicken broth or Low-Sodium Chicken Stock (variation, page 27)	1 L
1 cup	dark beer, such as amber or porter	250 mL
2 cups	shredded sharp (old) Cheddar cheese	500 mL
	Salt	

1. Set your Instant Pot to sauté on Normal. When the display says Hot, add butter and heat until melted. Add onions and cook, stirring often, for 5 minutes or until softened. Gradually add 2 tbsp (30 mL) flour, stirring until moistened. Season to taste with pepper; cook, stirring, for 1 minute. Gradually pour in broth, 1 cup (250 mL) at a time, stirring well to combine. Add beer, stirring well. Press Cancel.

2. Close and lock the lid and turn the steam release handle to Sealing. Set your Instant Pot to pressure cook on High for 5 minutes.

3. When the cooking time is done, press Cancel and let stand, covered, for 10 minutes, then turn the steam release handle to Venting. When the float valve drops down, remove the lid.

4. Place cheese in a bowl and sprinkle with the remaining flour, tossing to coat evenly.

5. Set your Instant Pot to sauté on Less. Add cheese, a handful at a time, and cook, stirring well to combine, until cheese is melted.

6. Using the immersion blender, purée soup until smooth. Season to taste with salt and pepper.

SERVING SUGGESTION

Serve garnished with popcorn or chopped fresh parsley.

VARIATION

If your local grocer sells mirepoix (a combination of finely chopped onions, carrots and celery), you can substitute about 1½ cups (375 mL) mirepoix for the onion in this recipe. Add the mirepoix in step 1 and cook until onions are softened. You can also make your own mirepoix following the instructions on page 19.

TO SLOW COOK

Complete step 1. In place of steps 2 and 3, close and lock the lid and turn the steam release handle to Venting. Set your Instant Pot to slow cook on Less for 8 hours or on More for 4 hours. When the cooking time is done, remove the lid. Continue with step 4.

TIP

In step 4, instead of using an immersion blender, you can transfer the soup, in batches, to a countertop blender. Be very careful when transferring soup, as it is very hot. Do not fill your blender more than halfway, to prevent hot soup from spewing out the top. After puréeing, return soup to the cooker. Set your Instant Pot to sauté on Less and cook, stirring, for 2 to 3 minutes or until warmed through.

Creamy Potato Leek Soup

If you are looking for a simple, yet versatile soup, this one will become a staple. Served warm, this classic soup will comfort you on cold and rainy days. Served chilled, it will refresh you on warm summer days.

MAKES 6 TO 8 SERVINGS

COOKING PROGRAMS

• Pressure Cook •
• Sauté •

• **Immersion blender (see tip)**

4	yellow-fleshed potatoes (about 2 lbs/1 kg), peeled and chopped	4
3	leeks (white part only), thinly sliced and rings separated	3
2	bay leaves	2
1 tbsp	chopped fresh thyme	15 mL
4 cups	ready-to-use chicken broth or Chicken Stock (page 27)	1 L
1½ cups	heavy or whipping (35%) cream	375 mL
	Salt and freshly ground black pepper	
	Chopped fresh chives (optional)	

1. In the inner pot, combine potatoes, leeks, bay leaves, thyme and broth, stirring well.

2. Close and lock the lid and turn the steam release handle to Sealing. Set your Instant Pot to pressure cook on High for 5 minutes.

3. When the cooking time is done, press Cancel and let stand, covered, until the float valve drops down. Remove the lid. The potatoes should be fork-tender. (If more cooking time is needed, continue pressure cooking on High for 1 minute, then quickly release the pressure.) Discard bay leaves.

4. Using the immersion blender, purée soup until smooth.

5. Set your Instant Pot to sauté on Less. Stir in cream and season to taste with salt and pepper; cook, stirring often, for 2 to 3 minutes or until heated through. Serve garnished with chives, if using.

TIPS

Leeks should be carefully washed before use, as they can be very sandy in between their layers. Pat dry with a paper towel after washing.

In step 4, instead of using an immersion blender, you can transfer the soup, in batches, to a countertop blender. Be very careful when transferring soup, as it is very hot. Do not fill your blender more than halfway, to prevent hot soup from spewing out the top. After puréeing, return soup to the cooker.

The soup can be stored in airtight containers in the refrigerator for up to 1 week or in the freezer for up to 3 months. Thaw in the refrigerator or defrost in the microwave. Reheat in a saucepan over medium heat, stirring occasionally, until warmed through.

For freezer storage, measure soup into serving-size portions and label the containers.

Fireside Tomato Soup

There is something so comforting about a bowl of creamy tomato soup, and this buttery, nuanced version is easy to make from scratch.

COOKING PROGRAMS

• Pressure Cook •
• Sauté •

- **Immersion blender (see tip)**

½ cup	loosely packed fresh basil leaves, chopped	125 mL
1 tsp	granulated sugar	5 mL
3¾ cups	ready-to-use reduced-sodium chicken broth or Low-Sodium Chicken Stock (variation, page 27)	925 mL
2	cans (each 14½ oz/411 mL) diced tomatoes with garlic and onion, with juice	2
1 cup	half-and-half (10%) cream	250 mL
¼ cup	butter, softened	60 mL
	Freshly ground black pepper	

1. To the inner pot, add basil, sugar, broth and tomatoes with juice. Do not stir (see tip).

2. Close and lock the lid and turn the steam release handle to Sealing. Set your Instant Pot to pressure cook on High for 5 minutes.

3. When the cooking time is done, press Cancel and let stand, covered, for 5 minutes, then turn the steam release handle to Venting. When the float valve drops down, remove the lid.

4. Using the immersion blender, purée soup until smooth.

5. Set your Instant Pot to sauté on Less. Stir in cream and butter; cook, stirring, for 2 to 3 minutes or until heated through (do not let boil). Season to taste with pepper.

TIPS

Substitute a can of fire-roasted tomatoes for 1 can of the diced tomatoes.

Do not be tempted to add the tomatoes first or to stir the ingredients. Tomatoes can scorch on the bottom of the cooker if added first.

In step 4, instead of using an immersion blender, you can transfer the soup, in batches, to a countertop blender. Be very careful when transferring soup, as it is very hot. Do not fill your blender more than halfway, to prevent hot soup from spewing out the top. After puréeing, return soup to the cooker.

Carrot and Ginger Soup

This mouthwatering soup is ideal as an appetizer or as a side dish with a sandwich. Its bright orange color is punctuated by the slightly spicy flavor of ginger and a nutty hint of coconut milk.

MAKES 4 TO 6 SERVINGS

COOKING PROGRAMS

• Sauté •
• Pressure Cook or Slow Cook •

• **Immersion blender (see tip)**

2 tbsp	virgin olive oil	30 mL
1 lb	carrots, chopped	500 g
1	onion, chopped	1
2 tsp	grated gingerroot	10 mL
4 cups	ready-to-use vegetable broth or Vegetable Stock (page 28)	1 L
½ cup	coconut milk	125 mL
	Salt and freshly ground black pepper	
1 to 2 tbsp	freshly squeezed lime or lemon juice	15 to 30 mL

1. Set your Instant Pot to sauté on More. When the display says Hot, add oil and heat until shimmering. Add carrots and onion; cook, stirring often, for 5 minutes or until onion is softened. Stir in ginger and cook, stirring, for 1 minute. Stir in broth. Press Cancel.

2. Close and lock the lid and turn the steam release handle to Sealing. Set your Instant Pot to pressure cook on High for 5 minutes.

3. When the cooking time is done, press Cancel and turn the steam release handle to Venting. When the float valve drops down, remove the lid. The carrots should be fork-tender. (If more cooking time is needed, continue pressure cooking on High for 1 minute.)

4. Using the immersion blender, purée soup until smooth. Stir in coconut milk. Season to taste with salt, pepper and lime juice.

TO SLOW COOK

Complete step 1, increasing broth to 4½ cups (1.125 L). In place of steps 2 and 3, close and lock the lid and turn the steam release handle to Venting. Set your Instant Pot to slow cook on Less for 8 hours. When the cooking time is done, remove the lid. The carrots should be fork-tender. (If more cooking time is needed, continue slow cooking on Less for 1 to 2 hours.) Continue with step 4.

For faster slow cooking, set your Instant Pot to slow cook on More for 3 to 4 hours or until carrots are fork-tender.

TIPS

In step 4, instead of using an immersion blender, you can transfer the soup, in batches, to a countertop blender. Be very careful when transferring soup, as it is very hot. Do not fill your blender more than halfway, to prevent hot soup from spewing out the top. After puréeing, return soup to the cooker. Set your Instant Pot to sauté on Less. Cook, stirring often, until heated through.

The soup can be stored in airtight containers in the refrigerator for up to 1 week or in the freezer for up to 3 months. Thaw in the refrigerator or defrost in the microwave. Reheat in a saucepan over medium heat, stirring occasionally, until warmed through.

For freezer storage, measure soup into serving-size portions and label the containers.

Super-Easy Beef Stew

A hearty beef stew is always a crowd-pleaser. Using a seasoning mix and precut beef and vegetables, this version is easy to put together on a moment's notice, giving you an easy dish for family gatherings or potlucks.

MAKES 6 SERVINGS

COOKING PROGRAMS

• Sauté •
• Pressure Cook •

2 lbs	beef stew meat, cut into 1½-inch (4 cm) cubes	1 kg
	Salt and freshly ground black pepper	
3 tbsp	vegetable oil (approx.), divided	45 mL
1	packet (1½ oz/43 g) beef stew seasoning mix, divided	1
2 cups	ready-to-use reduced-sodium beef broth or Low-Sodium Beef Bone Broth (page 26)	500 mL
3	carrots, cut into 1½-inch (4 cm) chunks	3
1 lb	small white potatoes, quartered	500 g
¼ cup	cold water	60 mL
3 tbsp	all-purpose flour	45 mL

1. Season beef lightly with salt and pepper. Set your Instant Pot to sauté on Normal. When the display says Hot, add 2 tbsp (30 mL) oil and heat until shimmering. Working in batches, add beef and cook, stirring, for 2 minutes or until browned on all sides, adding more oil as needed between batches. Using tongs or a slotted spoon, transfer beef to a plate as it is browned.

2. Add seasoning mix and broth to the pot; cook, stirring and scraping up any browned bits from the bottom of the pot, for 2 minutes. Return beef and any accumulated juices to the pot and stir in carrots and potatoes. Press Cancel.

3. Close and lock the lid and turn the steam release handle to Sealing. Set your Instant Pot to pressure cook on High for 20 minutes.

4. When the cooking time is done, press Cancel and let stand, covered, for 10 minutes, then turn the steam release handle to Venting. When the float valve drops down, remove the lid. The beef and vegetables should be fork-tender. (If more cooking time is needed, continue pressure cooking on High for 5 minutes.)

5. Add cold water to a small bowl and whisk in flour until smooth.

6. Set your Instant Pot to sauté on Normal. Slowly pour flour mixture into the pot and cook, stirring often, for 5 minutes or until stew is thickened to your liking. Season to taste with salt and pepper.

VARIATION

Add 1 onion, cut into thin wedges, with the carrots and potatoes in step 2.

TIPS

If serving this stew at a party, keep it in the pot on the Keep Warm setting. It can be kept warm for up to 2 hours.

The stew can be stored in airtight containers in the refrigerator for up to 3 days or in the freezer for up to 3 months.

Texas-Style Beef Chili

When you head down to Texas and the Southwest, make sure you don't mention beans when you talk about chili! What you will find in their version is hearty chunks of beef and a bit of a bite from chile peppers.

MAKES 4 SERVINGS

COOKING PROGRAMS

- Sauté •
- Pressure Cook •

2 lbs	beef stew meat, cut into 1½-inch (4 cm) cubes	1 kg
	Salt	
3 tbsp	vegetable oil (approx.), divided	45 mL
1 tbsp	chili powder	15 mL
2 tsp	ground cumin	10 mL
1½ cups	ready-to-use reduced-sodium beef broth or Low-Sodium Beef Bone Broth (page 26)	375 mL
2	chipotle peppers in 1½ tbsp (22 mL) adobo sauce, chopped	2
2 cups	chunky salsa	500 mL

1. Season beef with salt. Set your Instant Pot to sauté on Normal. When the display says Hot, add 2 tbsp (30 mL) oil and heat until shimmering. Working in batches, add beef and cook, stirring, for 3 to 5 minutes or until browned on all sides, adding more oil as needed between batches. Using tongs or a slotted spoon, transfer beef to a plate as it is browned.

2. Stir chili powder and cumin into the pot; cook, stirring, for 15 seconds. Add broth and cook for 2 minutes, scraping up any browned bits from the bottom of the pot. Return beef and any accumulated juices to the pot and stir in chipotle peppers with sauce and salsa. Press Cancel.

3. Close and lock the lid and turn the steam release handle to Sealing. Set your Instant Pot to pressure cook on High for 20 minutes.

4. When the cooking time is done, press Cancel and let stand, covered, for 10 minutes, then turn the steam release handle to Venting. When the float valve drops down, remove the lid. The beef should be fork-tender. (If more cooking time is needed, continue pressure cooking on High for 3 minutes.)

5. Set your Instant Pot to sauté on Normal. Cook, stirring often, for 5 to 10 minutes or until chili is thickened to your liking.

SERVING SUGGESTION

Serve tortilla chips on the side or crumble them over top.

TIPS

Cut your beef into pieces of a similar size, so they cook evenly.

The chili can be stored in airtight containers in the refrigerator for up to 3 days or in the freezer for up to 3 months. Thaw in the refrigerator or defrost in the microwave. Reheat in a saucepan over medium heat, stirring occasionally, until warmed through.

For freezer storage, measure chili into serving-size portions and label the containers.

Northern Beefy Chili

When it comes to chili, different regions think theirs is the best and the only "real" chili. While I may not be quite that impassioned, this version, served in many northern states, is the one I grew up with, and it's one of my favorites.

MAKES 8 SERVINGS

COOKING PROGRAMS

• Sauté •
• Pressure Cook or Slow Cook •

1 tbsp	vegetable oil	15 mL
1	onion, finely chopped	1
2 lbs	ground beef	1 kg
2 tbsp	chili powder	30 mL
3	cans (each 14½ oz/411 mL) diced tomatoes with green chiles, with juice	3
2	cans (each 14 to 19 oz/398 to 540 mL) red kidney beans, drained and rinsed	2
1 cup	ready-to-use reduced-sodium beef broth or Low-Sodium Beef Bone Broth (page 26)	250 mL
	Salt and freshly ground black pepper	

1. Set your Instant Pot to sauté on Normal. When the display says Hot, add oil and heat until shimmering. Add onion and cook, stirring, for 3 to 5 minutes or until translucent. Add beef and cook, breaking it up with a spoon, for 10 minutes or until no longer pink. Stir in chili powder, tomatoes with juice, beans and broth. Season to taste with salt and pepper. Press Cancel.

2. Close and lock the lid and turn the steam release handle to Sealing. Set your Instant Pot to pressure cook on High for 15 minutes.

3. When the cooking time is done, press Cancel and let stand, covered, for 15 minutes, then turn the steam release handle to Venting. When the float valve drops down, remove the lid. The flavors should be melded. (If more cooking time is needed, continue pressure cooking on High for 2 minutes, then quickly release the pressure.) Stir well and season to taste with salt and pepper.

SERVING SUGGESTION

Serve garnished with shredded cheese, sour cream, sliced green onions and/or chopped red onions.

TIPS

If you prefer, you can cook 1 cup (250 mL) dried red kidney beans, following the instructions on page 29, and use them in place of the canned beans.

For a spicier chili, add hot pepper sauce to taste at the end of step 3, or to individual servings.

TO SLOW COOK

Complete step 1, increasing broth to 1¼ cups (300 mL). In place of steps 2 and 3, close and lock the lid and turn the steam release handle to Venting. Set your Instant Pot to slow cook on Less for 6 to 8 hours, or on More for 3 to 4 hours, until the flavors are melded to your liking. Stir well.

Southwestern Pulled Pork Chili

Pork shoulder gets treated with a taco seasoning rub and is then partnered with green salsa and white beans for a two-stepping spicy chili that will keep you dancing.

MAKES 6 SERVINGS

COOKING PROGRAMS

• Sauté •
• Pressure Cook •

2 lbs	boneless pork shoulder blade roast, cut in half	1 kg
	Salt	
2 tbsp	vegetable oil	30 mL
2 tbsp	taco seasoning	30 mL
2 cups	ready-to-use reduced-sodium chicken broth or Low-Sodium Chicken Stock (variation, page 27), divided	500 mL
2 cups	salsa verde, divided	500 mL
1	can (14 to 19 oz/398 to 540 mL) cannellini (white kidney) or Great Northern beans, drained and rinsed	1

1. Season pork lightly with salt. Set your Instant Pot to sauté on Normal. When the display says Hot, add oil and heat until shimmering. Working in batches, add pork and cook, turning, for 5 minutes or until browned on all sides. Transfer pork to a plate as it is browned.

2. Add taco seasoning to the pot and cook, stirring, for 30 seconds. Add broth and scrape up any browned bits from the bottom of the pot. Stir in 1 cup (250 mL) salsa. Return pork and any accumulated juices to the pot, turning to coat. Press Cancel.

3. Close and lock the lid and turn the steam release handle to Sealing. Set your Instant Pot to pressure cook on High for 45 minutes.

4. When the cooking time is done, press Cancel and let stand, covered, until the float valve drops down. Remove the lid. The pork should be melt-in-your-mouth tender. (If more cooking time is needed, continue pressure cooking on High for 10 minutes, then quickly release the pressure.)

5. Transfer pork to a cutting board. Using two forks, shred pork into bite-size pieces, discarding excess fat.

6. Skim off and discard fat from sauce in pot. Stir in beans and salsa. Set your Instant Pot to sauté on Normal. Cook, stirring often, for 10 minutes or until beans are heated through and liquid is slightly reduced. Return pork and accumulated juices to the pot; cook, stirring often, for 2 to 3 minutes or until heated through. Season to taste with salt, if desired.

SERVING SUGGESTION

Serve garnished with dollops of sour cream and/or chopped fresh cilantro.

TIP

If you prefer, you can cook $3/4$ cup (175 mL) dried cannellini or Great Northern beans, following the instructions on page 29, and use them in place of the canned beans.

White Bean Chicken Chili

Here, traditional chicken chili gets a flavor boost from spicy, aromatic salsa verde. With your Instant Pot, you can make this chili completely from scratch or using ready-to-go ingredients — or somewhere in between.

MAKES 6 SERVINGS

COOKING PROGRAM

• Pressure Cook •

1½ cups	dried cannellini (white kidney) beans	375 mL
	Water	
3 cups	diced leftover rotisserie chicken (store-bought or see recipe, page 100)	750 mL
1 tsp	ground cumin	5 mL
1	bay leaf	1
3½ cups	ready-to-use chicken broth or Chicken Stock (page 28)	875 mL
2 cups	salsa verde	500 mL
	Salt and freshly ground black pepper	
	Hot pepper flakes (optional)	

1. Place beans in a large bowl, add 6 cups (1.5 L) cold water and let soak at room temperature for 8 hours or overnight. Drain and rinse beans.

2. In the inner pot, combine beans, chicken, cumin, bay leaf, broth and salsa. Season to taste with salt and pepper.

3. Close and lock the lid and turn the steam release handle to Sealing. Set your Instant Pot to pressure cook on High for 10 minutes.

4. When the cooking time is done, press Cancel and let stand, covered, until the float valve drops down. Remove the lid. The beans should be tender. (If more cooking time is needed, continue pressure cooking on High for 2 minutes, then quickly release the pressure.) Discard bay leaf.

5. If you prefer a thicker chili, use a potato masher to mash some of the beans and break up some of the chicken until the chili is your desired consistency. Season to taste with salt and pepper. If desired, sprinkle with hot pepper flakes.

SERVING SUGGESTION

Serve garnished with diced avocado, shredded cheese, sour cream and/or crumbled tortilla chips.

TIPS

Three cups (750 mL) diced chicken is equal to about 11 oz (330 g) cooked boneless skinless chicken.

The chili can be stored in airtight containers in the refrigerator for up to 3 days or in the freezer for up to 3 months. Thaw in the refrigerator or defrost in the microwave. Reheat in a saucepan over medium heat, stirring occasionally, until warmed through.

For freezer storage, measure chili into serving-size portions and label the containers.

Black Bean and Sweet Potato Chili

This quick vegetarian chili, full of black beans and sweet potatoes, is perfect for a family meal, or make a double batch and eat it for lunch the next day or freeze the extras for another night.

COOKING PROGRAMS
• Sauté •
• Pressure Cook •

2	cans (each 14 to 19 oz/398 to 540 mL) black beans, drained and rinsed	2
2 tbsp	virgin olive oil	30 mL
1	sweet potato, peeled and cut into ³⁄₄-inch (2 cm) cubes	1
2 tbsp	chili powder	30 mL
2 tsp	ground cumin	10 mL
	Salt and freshly ground black pepper	
1	can (14¹⁄₂ oz/411 mL) diced tomatoes with garlic and onion, with juice	1
1 cup	water	250 mL
	Lime wedges (optional)	

1. In a small bowl, mash ¹⁄₂ cup (125 mL) of the beans. Set aside.

2. Set your Instant Pot to sauté on Normal. When the display says Hot, add oil and heat until shimmering. Add sweet potato and cook, stirring, for 2 minutes. Stir in chili powder, cumin, ¹⁄₄ tsp (1 mL) salt and pepper to taste; cook, stirring, for 1 minute. Stir in mashed and whole beans, tomatoes with juice and water. Press Cancel.

3. Close and lock the lid and turn the steam release handle to Sealing. Set your Instant Pot to pressure cook on High for 8 minutes.

4. When the cooking time is done, press Cancel and turn the steam release handle to Venting. When the float valve drops down, remove the lid. The sweet potatoes should be fork-tender. (If more cooking time is needed, continue pressure cooking on High for 1 minute.)

5. Season to taste with more salt and pepper. Serve with lime wedges to squeeze over top, if desired.

TIPS

This recipe is meant for Instant Pots that are 6 quarts (6 L) or larger. If you are using a smaller cooker, cut the recipe in half. If doubling the recipe, make sure you do not fill the pot more than halfway.

The chili can be stored in airtight containers in the refrigerator for up to 3 days or in the freezer for up to 3 months. Thaw in the refrigerator or defrost in the microwave. Reheat in a saucepan over medium heat, stirring occasionally, until warmed through.

For freezer storage, measure chili into serving-size portions and label the containers.

Vegetarian Lentil Chili

When you want a chili that packs a punch, with both powerhouse nutrients from brown lentils and the spiciness of chipotle pepper and green chiles, give this version a try.

MAKES 6 SERVINGS

COOKING PROGRAMS

• Sauté •
• Pressure Cook or Slow Cook •

1 tbsp	vegetable oil	15 mL
½ cup	chopped red onion	125 mL
1½ cups	dried brown lentils, rinsed and drained	375 mL
2 tsp	chipotle chile powder	10 mL
1	can (28 oz/796 mL) diced tomatoes with mild green chiles, with juice	1
4 cups	ready-to-use reduced-sodium vegetable broth or Low-Sodium Vegetable Stock (variation, page 28)	1 L

1. Set your Instant Pot to sauté on Normal. When the display says Hot, add oil and heat until shimmering. Add onion and cook, stirring often, for 5 minutes or until softened. Stir in lentils, chile powder, tomatoes with juice and broth. Press Cancel.

2. Close and lock the lid and turn the steam release handle to Sealing. Set your Instant Pot to pressure cook on High for 10 minutes.

3. When the cooking time is done, press Cancel and let stand, covered, for 10 minutes, then turn the steam release handle to Venting. When the float valve drops down, remove the lid. The lentils should be tender. (If more cooking time is needed, continue pressure cooking on High for 2 minutes, then quickly release the pressure.)

SERVING SUGGESTION

Serve garnished with shredded cheese, sour cream and/or chopped red onions.

VARIATION

Meaty Lentil Chili: For meat lovers, in step 1 add 1 lb (500 g) lean ground beef with the onion and cook, stirring and breaking beef up with a spoon, until beef is no longer pink.

TO SLOW COOK

Complete step 1. In place of steps 2 and 3, close and lock the lid and turn the steam release handle to Venting. Set your Instant Pot to slow cook on Less for 4 hours. When the cooking time is done, remove the lid. The lentils should be tender. (If more cooking time is needed, continue slow cooking on Less for 1 to 2 hours.)

For faster slow cooking, set your Instant Pot to slow cook on More for 2 hours or until the beans are tender.

TIPS

You can adjust the amount of chipotle chile powder if you like more or less spiciness. If increasing the amount, add 1/2 tsp (2 mL) more at a time.

If you cannot find diced tomatoes with mild green chilies, you can use tomatoes with green peppers and/or garlic, or just plain diced tomatoes.

The chili can be stored in airtight containers in the refrigerator for up to 3 days or in the freezer for up to 3 months. Thaw in the refrigerator or defrost in the microwave. Reheat in a saucepan over medium heat, stirring occasionally, until warmed through.

For freezer storage, measure chili into serving-size portions and label the containers.

BEEF AND PORK

Coconut Curry Beef

Thai red curry paste adds interesting flavor notes to the beef chunks in this recipe without making it over-the-top spicy. Serve it with any of your favorite side dishes.

MAKES 4 SERVINGS		

COOKING PROGRAMS		
• Sauté •		
• Pressure Cook •		

1½ lb	beef brisket, cut into 1½-inch (4 cm) cubes	750 g
	Salt	
3 tbsp	coconut oil or vegetable oil (approx.)	45 mL
1	onion, finely chopped	1
2 tbsp	Thai red curry paste	30 mL
¾ cup	strained tomato purée (passata)	175 mL
1	can (14 oz/400 mL) coconut milk	1
2	green onions, sliced diagonally (optional)	2

1. Season beef with salt. Set your Instant Pot to sauté on Normal. When the display says Hot, add 2 tbsp (30 mL) oil and heat until shimmering. Working in batches, add beef and cook, stirring, for 3 to 5 minutes or until browned on all sides, adding more oil as needed between batches. Using a slotted spoon, transfer beef to a plate as it is browned.

2. Add onion to the fat remaining in the pot and cook, stirring often, for 3 minutes or until translucent. Add curry paste and cook, stirring, for 1 minute or until fragrant. Stir in tomato purée, scraping up any browned bits from the bottom of the pot. Press Cancel. Return beef and any accumulated juices to the pot, stirring well.

3. Close and lock the lid and turn the steam release handle to Sealing. Set your Instant Pot to pressure cook on High for 35 minutes.

4. When the cooking time is done, press Cancel and turn the steam release handle to Venting. When the float valve drops down, remove the lid. The beef should be fork-tender. (If more cooking time is needed, continue pressure cooking on High for 3 minutes.)

5. Set your Instant Pot to sauté on Normal. Add coconut milk and cook, stirring, for 5 minutes or until sauce is thickened to your liking. Season to taste with salt. Serve garnished with green onions, if using.

SERVING SUGGESTION

Serve over Foolproof Jasmine Rice (page 32) or Super-Simple Brown Rice (page 31).

TIP

Buy the best-quality coconut milk you can find for the best results in this curry. Check the ingredients and choose one with coconut milk (not water) listed first.

Pepperoncini Beef Roast

This mouthwateringly tender beef roast is satisfying and packed with flavor. Whether you cook it fast or slow, three simple pantry ingredients make it so easy that it's sure to be a favorite addition to your family's meals.

MAKES 6 SERVINGS

COOKING PROGRAM

• Pressure Cook or Slow Cook •

3 lb	boneless beef chuck roast (less than 8 inches/20 cm in diameter)	1.5 kg
	Salt and freshly ground black pepper	
4	pepperoncini peppers	4
5 tsp	ranch dressing mix (about two-thirds of a 1-oz/28 g packet)	25 mL
5 tsp	au jus gravy mix (about half of a 1-oz/28 g packet)	25 mL
1½ cups	water	375 mL

1. Season roast with salt and pepper. Place roast in the inner pot and arrange peppers on top.

2. In a medium bowl, whisk together ranch dressing, gravy mix and water. Pour over roast.

3. Close and lock the lid and turn the steam release handle to Sealing. Set your Instant Pot to pressure cook on High for 45 minutes.

4. When the cooking time is done, press Cancel and let stand, covered, for 10 minutes, then turn the steam release handle to Venting. When the float valve drops down, remove the lid. The roast should be fork-tender. (If more cooking time is needed, continue pressure cooking on High for 5 minutes, then quickly release the pressure.)

5. Using a slotted spoon, remove peppers from pot and set aside. Using tongs, transfer roast to a cutting board, cover with foil and let stand for 5 minutes.

6. Slice roast across the grain and transfer slices to a serving platter. Skim off fat from cooking liquid and drizzle roast with some of the liquid. Arrange peppers around roast.

VARIATION

Replace the water with ready-to-use reduced-sodium beef broth or Low-Sodium Beef Bone Broth (page 26). Unless using no-salt-added broth or stock, do not season roast with salt.

TO SLOW COOK

Complete steps 1 and 2. In place of steps 3 and 4, close and lock the lid and turn the steam release handle to Venting. Set your Instant Pot to slow cook on Less for 7 hours. When the cooking time is done, remove the lid. The roast should be fork-tender. (If more cooking time is needed, continue slow cooking on Less for 1 to 2 hours.) Continue with step 5.

For faster slow cooking, set your Instant Pot to slow cook on More for 3 to 4 hours or until the roast is tender and no longer pink inside.

Creamy Beef Stroganoff

Some dishes withstand the test of time, and this classic combination of beef, onions, mushrooms and sour cream coalesced into a rich and chunky gravy served over wide noodles is certainly one of them. You can make it fast or slow; either way, the result is mouthwatering goodness.

MAKES 6 SERVINGS

COOKING PROGRAMS

• Sauté •
• Pressure Cook or Slow Cook •

1½ lb	boneless beef chuck roast, cut into 1½-inch (4 cm) pieces	750 g
	Salt and freshly ground black pepper	
3 tbsp	virgin olive oil (approx.)	45 mL
¼ cup	butter	60 mL
1	large onion, cut in half, sliced and rings separated	1
1 lb	mushrooms, sliced	500 g
1½ cups	ready-to-use reduced-sodium beef broth or Low-Sodium Beef Bone Broth (page 26)	375 mL
12 oz	broad egg noodles	375 g
1 cup	sour cream	250 mL

1. Season beef with salt and pepper. Set your Instant Pot to sauté on Normal. When the display says Hot, add 2 tbsp (30 mL) oil and heat until shimmering. Working in batches, add beef and cook, stirring, for 3 to 5 minutes or until browned on all sides, adding more oil as needed between batches. Using a slotted spoon, transfer beef to a plate as it is browned.

2. Add butter to the pot and heat until melted. Add onion and mushrooms; cook, stirring, for about 15 minutes or until onion and mushrooms are softened and liquid is evaporated. Stir in broth. Press Cancel. Return beef and any accumulated juices to the pot, stirring well.

3. Close and lock the lid and turn the steam release handle to Sealing. Set your Instant Pot to pressure cook on High for 20 minutes.

4. Meanwhile, in a large pot of boiling salted water, cook egg noodles according to package directions. Drain and set aside.

5. When the cooking time is done, press Cancel and turn the steam release handle to Venting. When the float valve drops down, remove the lid. The beef should be fork-tender. (If more cooking time is needed, continue pressure cooking on High for 3 minutes.)

6. If you prefer a thicker sauce, set your Instant Pot to sauté on Normal. Cook, stirring, for about 5 minutes or until sauce is the desired consistency. Press Cancel.

7. Stir sour cream into sauce and season to taste with salt and pepper. Serve beef mixture over noodles.

TO SLOW COOK

Complete steps 1 and 2, reducing the butter to 1 tbsp (15 mL) and omitting the mushrooms and broth. In a small bowl, combine 2 cans (each 10 oz/284 mL) condensed cream of mushroom soup and 1 cup (250 mL) milk. Stir into pot before returning the beef. In place of steps 3 and 5, close and lock the lid and turn the steam release handle to Venting. Set your Instant Pot to slow cook on Less for 8 hours. When the cooking time is done, remove the lid. The beef should be fork-tender. (If more cooking time is needed, continue slow cooking on Less for 1 to 2 hours.) Meanwhile, complete step 4. When the beef is fork-tender, continue with step 6.

For faster slow cooking, set your Instant Pot to slow cook on More for 4 to 5 hours or until beef is fork-tender.

TIPS

You can use garlic salt in place of plain salt.

Instead of the sour cream, try Homemade Yogurt (page 54).

When using the Quick Release method to release pressure, keep your hands and face away from the hole on top of the steam release handle so you don't get scalded by the escaping steam.

Easy Colorado Burritos

When you can serve up a dish that is so easy to make, yet so wildly satisfying, you'll want to keep the recipe bookmarked to make again and again.

MAKES 8 SERVINGS

COOKING PROGRAM

• Pressure Cook •

- **13- by 9-inch (33 by 23 cm) glass baking dish, sprayed with nonstick cooking spray**

3 lb	boneless beef chuck (blade) roast, cut into 3 pieces	1.5 kg
2 cups	red enchilada sauce, divided	500 mL
½ cup	ready-to-use reduced-sodium beef broth or Low-Sodium Beef Bone Broth (page 26)	125 mL
2 tbsp	Worcestershire sauce	30 mL
8	large (10-inch/25 cm) flour tortillas	8
2½ cups	shredded Monterey Jack cheese, divided	625 mL

1. In the inner pot, combine beef, 1 cup (250 mL) enchilada sauce, broth and Worcestershire sauce.

2. Close and lock the lid and turn the steam release handle to Sealing. Set your Instant Pot to pressure cook on High for 40 minutes.

3. When the cooking time is done, press Cancel and let stand, covered, for 10 minutes, then turn the steam release handle to Venting. When the float valve drops down, remove the lid. The beef should be fork-tender and no longer pink in the middle. (If more cooking time is needed, continue pressure cooking on High for 5 minutes, then quickly release the pressure.)

4. Using tongs, transfer beef to a cutting board. Shred beef with two forks or cut into small pieces, discarding excess fat. Spoon off fat from sauce in pot. Return beef to sauce, stirring well.

5. Place 1 tortilla on a plate and, using a slotted spoon, spoon about ⅔ cup (150 mL) beef mixture into the center. Sprinkle with 2½ tbsp (37 mL) cheese. Fold in bottom and sides of tortilla and roll up. Place seam side down in prepared baking dish. Repeat with the remaining tortillas, beef mixture and cheese, arranging rolled burritos alongside each other. Discard liquid from pot.

6. Preheat oven to 425°F (220°C).

7. Pour the remaining enchilada sauce lengthwise down the center of the burritos. Sprinkle remaining cheese on top of sauce.

8. Bake, uncovered, for 10 minutes or until cheese is melted.

TIPS

Leftover burritos can be stored in an airtight container in the refrigerator for up to 3 days.

To make and freeze burritos ahead of time, complete recipe through step 5. Wrap individual burritos in freezer-safe plastic wrap or bags and freeze for up to 3 months. Thaw in the microwave or overnight in the refrigerator. Continue with step 6.

Add a 16-oz (435 g) can of refried beans, spreading some evenly down the center of each tortilla before adding the beef mixture in step 5.

Juicy No-Grill Hamburgers

When you're craving a mouthwatering hamburger but either don't have a grill or don't want to fire it up, your Instant Pot comes to the rescue. Wrapped in foil and done in a flash, these burgers turn out juicy and seasoned to perfection.

MAKES 4 SERVINGS

COOKING PROGRAM
• Pressure Cook •

- **4 sheets of foil**
- **Steam rack**

1¼ lbs	lean ground beef	625 g
4 tsp	dried onion flakes	20 mL
1 tsp	salt	5 mL
¾ tsp	freshly ground black pepper	3 mL
1 tbsp	Worcestershire sauce	15 mL
4	hamburger buns, split and toasted	4

1. In a medium bowl, using your hands, combine beef, onion flakes, salt, pepper and Worcestershire sauce. Form into four ½-inch (1 cm) thick patties. Transfer each patty to a foil sheet and fold into flat packets (see page 13), sealing edges tightly.

2. Add 1¼ cups (300 mL) hot water to the inner pot and place the steam rack in the pot. Arrange packets on the rack, stacking them in alternating layers (like stacking bricks).

3. Close and lock the lid and turn the steam release handle to Sealing. Set your Instant Pot to pressure cook on High for 6 minutes.

4. When the cooking time is done, press Cancel and turn the steam release handle to Venting. When the float valve drops down, remove the lid and carefully open a packet. An instant-read thermometer inserted horizontally into the center of the patty should register at least 160°F (71°C). (If more cooking time is needed, continue pressure cooking on High for 1 minute.) Using tongs, transfer packets to a work surface and let stand for 5 minutes.

5. Carefully open packets, pour off liquid and transfer patties to buns.

SERVING SUGGESTIONS

Top the burgers with your favorite condiments, such as ketchup, mustard, mayonnaise, lettuce, sliced tomato, sliced onion and sliced pickles or relish.

Top the patties with slices of sharp (old) Cheddar, provolone, Monterey Jack, pepper Jack or crumbled blue cheese immediately after placing the patties on the bottom halves of the buns. Finish with the desired condiments.

Top the patties with cooked bacon slices and finish with the desired condiments.

TIP
Open the foil packets carefully to avoid getting burned by steam and spilling the residual juices.

Rosemary and Apple Pork Roast

Smothered in an apple, onion and rosemary gravy, this tender pork loin roast is a gratifying addition to your Sunday dinner table.

COOKING PROGRAMS

- Sauté -
- Pressure Cook -

1½ lb	boneless pork single loin roast (less than 8 inches/20 cm long), untied	750 g
	Salt and freshly ground black pepper	
2 tbsp	virgin olive oil	30 mL
2	small tart green apples (such as Granny Smith), peeled and chopped	2
1	onion, chopped	1
2	cloves garlic, peeled (optional)	2
2	sprigs fresh rosemary	2
1 cup	ready-to-use reduced-sodium chicken broth or Low-Sodium Chicken Stock (variation, page 27)	250 mL
2 tbsp	all-purpose flour	30 mL
¼ cup	water	60 mL

TIPS

Make sure to purchase a pork loin roast and not a pork tenderloin, which would not provide the intended results.

You can use any apples with a tart flavor, such as Cortland, Empire or Honeycrisp.

1. Season roast with ¼ tsp (1 mL) salt and pepper to taste. Set your Instant Pot to sauté on Normal. When the display says Hot, add oil and heat until shimmering. Add roast and cook, turning, for about 7 minutes or until browned on all sides. Press Cancel. Stir in apples, onion, garlic (if using) and rosemary to coat in oil, then stir in broth.

2. Close and lock the lid and turn the steam release handle to Sealing. Set your Instant Pot to pressure cook on High for 12 minutes.

3. When the cooking time is done, press Cancel and let stand, covered, for 5 minutes, then turn the steam release handle to venting. When the float valve drops down, remove the lid. An instant-read thermometer inserted in the thickest part of the roast should register at least 150°F (66°C) for medium. (If more cooking time is needed, continue pressure cooking on High for 2 minutes, then quickly release the pressure.)

4. Using tongs, transfer roast to a cutting board and tent with foil to keep warm.

5. Place flour in a small bowl and whisk in flour to make a slurry.

6. Set your Instant Pot to sauté on Normal. Pour in slurry, whisking to combine. Cook, whisking, for 2 to 3 minutes or until thickened. Discard rosemary stems. Season to taste with salt and pepper.

7. Cut pork across the grain into ½-inch (1 cm) thick slices. Transfer pork slices to a serving platter and serve with gravy.

Honey Dijon Pork Tenderloin

The sweet and savory duo of honey and mustard gives pork just the right amount of pizzazz.

MAKES 8 SERVINGS

COOKING PROGRAMS

• Pressure Cook •
• Sauté •

- **Rimmed baking sheet, lined with heavy-duty foil**

2	pork tenderloins (each about 1 lb/500 g)	2
	Salt and freshly ground black pepper	
3 tbsp	packed brown sugar	45 mL
2 tbsp	liquid honey	30 mL
2 tbsp	Dijon mustard	30 mL
1 tbsp	orange juice	15 mL
3/4 cup	ready-to-use chicken broth or Chicken Stock (page 27)	175 mL

1. Season pork with salt and pepper. Place pork in the inner pot, tucking the thin end under each tenderloin to create an even thickness.

2. In a small bowl, combine brown sugar, honey, mustard and orange juice. Add 1/4 cup (60 mL) of the honey-mustard mixture to the broth, stirring well. Pour over pork. Reserve the remaining honey-mustard mixture.

3. Close and lock the lid and turn the steam release handle to Sealing. Set your Instant Pot to pressure cook on High for 4 minutes.

4. When the cooking time is done, press Cancel and let stand, covered, for 5 minutes, then turn the steam release handle to Venting. When the float valve drops down, remove the lid. An instant-read thermometer inserted in the thickest part of a tenderloin should register at least 155°F (68°C) for medium-rare to medium. (If more cooking time is needed, continue pressure cooking on High for 1 minute, then quickly release the pressure.) Transfer tenderloins to prepared baking sheet, cover with foil and let stand for 10 minutes.

5. Meanwhile, preheat broiler, with the rack about 6 inches (15 mL) from the heat.

6. Brush reserved honey-mustard mixture over tenderloins, coating them all over. Space tenderloins apart, keeping the thin ends tucked under. Broil for 2 to 3 minutes or until glaze is caramelized.

7. Meanwhile, set your Instant Pot to sauté on Normal. Cook sauce, stirring often, until reduced by half.

8. Using tongs, transfer tenderloins to a cutting board and slice across the grain into medallions. Drizzle with sauce.

> **TIP**
> Be sure to purchase pork tenderloin and not pork loin, which would need a very different cooking time.

Maple Dijon Pork Medallions

Pressure cooking gives you juicy, tender pork tenderloin in minutes, and the maple mustard sauce adds just the right touch.

MAKES 4 SERVINGS

COOKING PROGRAMS

• Sauté •
• Pressure Cook •

1 lb	pork tenderloin, trimmed and cut in half crosswise	500 g
	Salt and freshly ground black pepper	
2 tbsp	vegetable oil	30 mL
3 tbsp	apple cider vinegar	45 mL
⅔ cup	ready-to-use reduced-sodium chicken broth or Low-Sodium Chicken Stock (variation, page 27)	150 mL
¼ cup	pure maple syrup	60 mL
2 tsp	Dijon mustard	10 mL
1 tbsp	butter	15 mL

1. Season pork with salt and pepper. Set your Instant Pot to sauté on Normal. When the display says Hot, add oil and heat until shimmering. Add pork and cook, turning often, for 5 minutes or until browned on all sides. Using tongs, transfer pork to a plate.

2. Carefully add vinegar to the pot and cook, scraping up any browned bits from the bottom of the pot, for 1 minute. Press Cancel. Add broth, maple syrup and mustard, stirring well. Return pork and any accumulated juices to the pot.

3. Close and lock the lid and turn the steam release handle to Sealing. Set your Instant Pot to pressure cook on Low for 2 minutes.

4. When the cooking time is done, press Cancel and let stand, covered, for 5 minutes, then turn the steam release handle to Venting. When the float valve drops down, remove the lid. An instant-read thermometer inserted in the thickest part of a tenderloin piece should register at least 155°F (68°C) for medium-rare to medium. (If more cooking time is needed, continue pressure cooking on Low for 2 minutes, then quickly release the pressure.) Using tongs, transfer pork to a cutting board, tent with foil and let rest until sauce is finished.

5. Set your Instant Pot to sauté on Less. Add butter and cook, stirring often, for 2 minutes or until butter is melted and combined.

6. Slice pork across the grain into medallions. Serve drizzled with maple mustard sauce.

SERVING SUGGESTION

Serve with rice pilaf and steamed vegetables for a simple yet decadent meal.

TIPS

Be sure to purchase pork tenderloin and not pork loin, which would need a very different cooking time.

Use long tongs to turn the pork tenderloin in step 1, to prevent burns from spattering oil.

Rosemary and Fig Pork Chops

Pork loin chops consistently turn out moist and tender in the pressure cooker. The sweet and tangy sauce adds a flavor twist that will make this dish one of your new favorites.

MAKES 4 SERVINGS

COOKING PROGRAMS
• Sauté •
• Pressure Cook •

4	boneless pork loin chops, about 1 inch (2.5 cm) thick (see tips, page 89)	4
	Salt and freshly ground black pepper	
2 tbsp	vegetable oil (approx.)	30 mL
1 cup	reduced-sodium ready-to-use chicken broth or Low-Sodium Chicken Stock (variation, page 27)	250 mL
3 tbsp	balsamic vinegar	45 mL
1/4 cup	finely chopped dried figs	60 mL
1 tsp	chopped fresh rosemary	5 mL
1 1/2 tbsp	liquid honey	22 mL
2 tbsp	butter, quartered	30 mL

1. Season pork with salt and pepper. Set your Instant Pot to sauté on More. When the display says Hot, add 1 tbsp (15 mL) oil and heat until shimmering. Working in batches, add chops and cook, turning once, for 2 minutes per side or until browned on both sides, adding more oil as needed between batches. Using tongs, transfer chops to a plate as they are browned.

2. Stir broth into the pot and bring to a simmer, scraping up any browned bits from the bottom. Return chops and any accumulated juices to the pot. Press Cancel.

3. Close and lock the lid and turn the steam release handle to Sealing. Set your Instant Pot to pressure cook on High for 3 minutes.

4. When the cooking time is done, press Cancel and turn the steam release handle to Venting. When the float valve drops down, remove the lid. An instant-read thermometer inserted horizontally into the thickest part of a chop should register 145°F (63°C) and the pork should be no longer pink but still juicy. (If more cooking time is needed, continue pressure cooking on High for 1 minute.) Using tongs, transfer chops to a platter and tent with foil.

5. Set your Instant Pot to sauté on Normal. Add vinegar and cook, stirring occasionally, for 5 minutes or until liquid is reduced by half. Stir in figs, rosemary and honey; cook, stirring often, for 2 minutes or until sauce is reduced by half. Stir in butter until melted. Return chops and any accumulated juices to the pot and turn to coat in sauce.

6. Transfer chops to a serving platter and spoon sauce over top. Serve immediately.

> **TIP**
> The pork chops may not be as pink in the middle as you are used to when cooking to medium-rare using a dry cooking method, but they will still be very juicy and tender.

Pork Chops with Stuffing and Gravy

Dinner for two is served up scrumptiously with these tender pork chops, stuffing and gravy, cooked using a pot-in-pot technique that keeps the stuffing fluffy. Drippings from the chops make for a rich gravy that ties the meal together.

MAKES 2 SERVINGS

COOKING PROGRAMS

- Sauté •
- Pressure Cook •

- **4-cup (1 L) round casserole dish**
- **Steam rack**

2 cups	herb-seasoned cubed stuffing (see tips)	500 mL
2	boneless pork loin chops, about 1 inch (2.5 cm) thick (see tips)	2
	Salt and freshly ground black pepper	
1 tbsp	vegetable oil	15 mL
2 cups	ready-to-use chicken broth or Chicken Stock (page 27)	500 mL
¼ cup	butter, melted	60 mL
3	sprigs fresh thyme	3
1 tsp	paprika	5 mL
1 tbsp	cornstarch	15 mL
3 tbsp	water	45 mL

1. Add stuffing to casserole dish. Set aside.

2. Season pork with salt and pepper. Set your Instant Pot to sauté on More. Add oil and heat until shimmering. Add chops and cook, turning once, for 2 minutes per side or until browned on both sides. Using tongs, transfer chops to a plate.

3. Add broth to the pot and bring to a simmer, scraping up any browned bits from the bottom. Press Cancel.

4. Remove ⅔ cup (150 mL) broth, stir in butter and pour over stuffing, stirring gently to coat.

5. Add thyme and paprika to the pot, stirring well. Return chops and any accumulated juices to the pot. Place steam rack over chops. Place casserole dish on rack.

6. Close and lock the lid and turn the steam release handle to Sealing. Set your Instant Pot to pressure cook on High for 3 minutes.

7. When the cooking time is done, press Cancel and turn the steam release handle to Venting. When the float valve drops down, remove the lid. Using the handles of the rack, carefully remove the rack and dish. An instant-read thermometer inserted horizontally into the thickest part of a chop should register at least 145°F (63°C), the pork should be no longer pink but still juicy, and the stuffing should fluff easily with a fork. (If more cooking time is needed, continue pressure cooking on High for 1 minute.) Using tongs, transfer chops to a clean plate. Discard thyme.

8. In a small bowl, whisk together cornstarch and water.

9. Set your Instant Pot to sauté on Normal. Slowly whisk cornstarch mixture into broth and cook, stirring, for 2 to 3 minutes or until thickened as desired. Season to taste with salt and pepper.

10. Serve pork with stuffing and gravy.

TIPS

Herb-seasoned stuffing cubes (such as Pepperidge Farm) are found in bags in the grocery store. If the packaged cubes are not available, you can use a crumblike stuffing (such as Stove Top).

To make your own stuffing cubes for this recipe, cut 4 slices of herb-seasoned bread into 3/4-inch (2 cm) cubes. Preheat oven to 275°F (140°C), with rack placed in the lower middle. Place cubes on a rimmed baking sheet and bake, stirring often, for about 50 minutes or until lightly browned and dry. Let cool to room temperature before use.

To prevent your chops from curling up at the edges, before browning, make a few tiny cuts in the fat and skin around the edges, without cutting into the meat.

When turning pork chops, use tongs to lift a portion of each chop up to see if it readily releases from the pot and is nicely browned. If not, cook for another 30 to 60 seconds before turning.

The pork chops may not be as pink in the middle as you are used to when cooking to medium-rare using a dry cooking method, but they will still be very juicy and tender.

Oniony Pulled Pork Sandwiches

If you love onions, get ready to dive right into these mouthwatering pulled pork sandwiches. Leftover pulled pork can be used to make tacos or poutine (see serving suggestion), or served up with a little barbecue sauce in a second round of sandwiches.

MAKES 8 SERVINGS

COOKING PROGRAMS

• Sauté •
• Pressure Cook or Slow Cook •

3½ lb	boneless pork shoulder blade roast	1.75 kg
2 tsp	freshly ground black pepper	10 mL
1½ tsp	salt	7 mL
2 tbsp	vegetable oil (approx.)	30 mL
2	sweet onions (such as Vidalia), coarsely chopped	2
4	cloves garlic, minced	4
1½ cups	ready-to-use chicken broth or Chicken Stock (page 27)	375 mL
1 tbsp	apple cider vinegar or sherry vinegar	15 mL
8	sandwich buns, split	8

1. Cut roast into 2 pieces that will fit easily inside the pot. Pat pork dry. Rub pork all over with pepper and salt.

2. Set your Instant Pot to sauté on Normal. When the display says Hot, add 1 tbsp (15 mL) oil and heat until shimmering. Working with one piece at a time, add pork and cook, turning, for 8 minutes or until browned on all sides, adding more oil as needed between batches. Using tongs, transfer pork to a plate as it is browned.

3. Add onions to the fat remaining in the pot and cook, stirring often, for 5 minutes or until softened. Add garlic and cook, stirring, for 1 minute or until fragrant. Press Cancel. Stir in broth and vinegar. Return pork and any accumulated juices to the pot, turning to coat.

4. Close and lock the lid and turn the steam release handle to Sealing. Set your Instant Pot to pressure cook on High for 60 minutes.

5. When the cooking time is done, press Cancel and let stand, covered, until the float valve drops down. Remove the lid. The pork should be fork-tender. (If more cooking time is needed, continue pressure cooking on High for 5 minutes, then quickly release the pressure.)

6. Transfer pork to a cutting board and, using two forks, shred pork. Discard any excess fat.

7. Place a colander over a large bowl and strain onions, reserving cooking liquid if you plan to store leftovers (see tip) or discarding it if you don't.

8. Meanwhile, toast the buns.

9. Divide shredded pork among sandwich buns. Serve topped with onions.

SERVING SUGGESTION

Use extra pulled pork to make poutine. Reheat pulled pork (with onions, if desired) as described in the tip. Pile hot french fries on a plate and sprinkle with cheese curds. Cover with pulled pork and ladle hot gravy evenly over top. Let stand for a few minutes to melt the cheese curds.

TIP

Leftover pulled pork can be refrigerated in airtight containers in some of the cooking liquid (with or without onions) for up to 3 days or frozen for up to 3 months. Thaw overnight in the refrigerator or defrost in the microwave. To reheat in the Instant Pot, set it to sauté on Normal and cook the pork, stirring occasionally, until heated through. Or reheat in the microwave or in a saucepan over medium heat. Drain pork and discard cooking liquid after reheating.

TO SLOW COOK

Complete steps 1 to 3. In place of steps 4 and 5, close and lock the lid and turn the steam release handle to Venting. Set your Instant Pot to slow cook on Normal for 8 hours. When the cooking time is done, remove the lid. The pork should be fork-tender. (If more cooking time is needed, continue slow cooking on Normal for 1 to 2 hours.) Continue with step 6.

For faster slow cooking, set your Instant Pot to slow cook on More for 4 to 5 hours or until pork is forktender.

Bavarian Pork Hocks and Kraut

This traditional dish, called *schweinhaxe* in German, is what you see served in overflowing dishes by dirndl-clad ladies at Oktoberfest. It takes meaty and succulent pork hocks, seasons them to perfection and then slathers them with sauerkraut.

MAKES 4 SERVINGS

COOKING PROGRAMS
• Sauté •
• Pressure Cook •

3 tbsp	vegetable oil (approx.)	45 mL
4	pork hocks	4
2	onions, quartered	2
10	black peppercorns, slightly crushed	10
2	bay leaves	2
3 cups	water	750 mL
1	jar (28 oz/796 mL) Bavarian-style sauerkraut with caraway seeds, with juice	1

1. Set your Instant Pot to sauté on Normal. When the display says Hot, add 2 tbsp (30 mL) oil and heat until shimmering. Working in batches, add hocks and cook, turning, for 5 minutes or until browned on all sides, adding more oil as needed between batches. Using tongs, transfer hocks to a plate as they are browned. Press Cancel.

2. Add onions, peppercorns, bay leaves and water to the pot. Return hocks and any accumulated juices to the pot.

3. Close and lock the lid and turn the steam release handle to Sealing. Set your Instant Pot to pressure cook on High for 33 minutes.

4. When the cooking time is done, press Cancel and turn the steam release handle to Venting. When the float valve drops down, remove the lid. The hocks should be fork-tender. (If more cooking time is needed, continue pressure cooking on High for 4 minutes.)

5. Using tongs, transfer hocks to a plate. Using a slotted spoon, remove and discard onions. Skim off any fat from the liquid in the pot. Discard all but 2/3 cup (150 mL) liquid. Return hocks to the pot and pour sauerkraut, with juice, over hocks.

6. Close and lock the lid and turn the steam release handle to Sealing. Set your Instant Pot to pressure cook on Low for 8 minutes.

7. When the cooking time is done, press Cancel and turn the steam release handle to Venting. When the float valve drops down, remove the lid. The sauerkraut should be tender and heated through. (If more cooking time is needed, continue pressure cooking on Low for 1 minute.) Discard bay leaves.

8. Transfer hocks to serving plates and spoon sauerkraut alongside.

> **TIPS**
>
> Be careful to avoid getting burned when turning the hocks in step 1; the skin and fat from the hocks can cause the oil to spit.
>
> You can substitute regular sauerkraut for the Bavarian-style sauerkraut, if desired.

Finger-Lickin' BBQ Ribs

No grill? No problem. You'll still achieve stellar results with this version of fall-off-the-bone tender ribs. They are worthy of company or an easy weeknight dinner.

MAKES 4 TO 6 SERVINGS

COOKING PROGRAMS

- Pressure Cook -
- Slow Cook -

2	slabs baby back pork ribs (4 to 6 lbs/2 to 3 kg total)	2
2 tbsp	Montreal steak seasoning	30 mL
2 cups	barbecue sauce, divided	500 mL
1 cup	water	250 mL
1	onion, chopped	1
¾ cup	apple preserves	175 mL

1. Cut ribs into 3- to 4-bone sections and season with steak seasoning.

2. In the inner pot, combine ½ cup (125 mL) barbecue sauce and water, stirring well. Stir in onion. Arrange ribs, standing on cut ends of bones, on top.

3. Close and lock the lid and turn the steam release handle to Sealing. Set your Instant Pot to pressure cook on High for 35 minutes.

4. When the cooking time is done, press Cancel and let stand, covered, for 10 minutes, then turn the steam release handle to Venting. When the float valve drops down, remove the lid. The ribs should be fork-tender. (If more cooking time is needed, continue pressure cooking on High for 5 minutes, then quickly release the pressure.)

5. In a medium bowl, combine apple preserves and the remaining barbecue sauce. Brush ribs with sauce.

6. Close and lock the lid and turn the steam release handle to Venting. Set your Instant Pot to slow cook on Less for 30 minutes.

7. When the cooking time is done, press Cancel. Transfer ribs to a serving platter and serve immediately.

VARIATIONS

Replace the apple preserves with peach, apricot or plum preserves.

For a darker glaze and stickier ribs, preheat the broiler with the rack 6 inches (15 cm) from the heat. After step 4, transfer ribs to a baking sheet lined with foil. Follow step 5, then, in place of step 6, broil ribs for 5 minutes. Serve immediately.

TO SLOW COOK ALONE

Complete steps 1 and 2. In place of steps 3 and 4, close and lock the lid and turn the steam release handle to Venting. Set your Instant Pot to slow cook on Less for 6 hours. When the cooking time is done, remove the lid. The ribs should be fork-tender. (If more cooking time is needed, continue slow cooking on Less for 1 to 2 hours.) Continue with step 5.

TIP

In step 6 (and in the alternative slow cooking method), you can cover the pot with the Instant Pot glass lid instead of the pressure cooking lid, if you prefer.

Vietnamese Pork Ribs

Here, mouthwatering spare ribs are coated in a caramel-like sauce combined with green onions and garlic for an added pick-me-up. Fish sauce brings the whole dish to a new level of umami.

MAKES 8 SERVINGS		

COOKING PROGRAMS		
• Pressure Cook • • Sauté •		

4 lbs	bone-in pork spare (side) ribs, cut into sections	2 kg
	Water	
1 tbsp	vegetable oil	15 mL
¼ cup	granulated sugar	60 mL
3	green onions, white and light green parts only, sliced	3
3	cloves garlic, minced	3
¾ cup	ready-to-use reduced-sodium chicken broth or Low-Sodium Chicken Stock (variation, page 27)	175 mL
2 tsp	fish sauce	10 mL
	Salt and freshly ground black pepper	

1. Arrange ribs in the inner pot and add enough water to just cover them. Close and lock the lid and turn the steam release handle to Sealing. Set your Instant Pot to pressure cook on High for 1 minute.

2. When the cooking time is done, press Cancel and let stand, covered, for 10 minutes, then turn the steam release handle to Venting. When the float valve drops down, remove the lid. Transfer ribs to a colander and rinse with cold water. Set aside. Discard liquid from pot. Rinse and dry pot and return to cooker.

3. Set your Instant Pot to sauté on Normal. When the display says Hot, add oil, turning pot to coat bottom. Add sugar and ¼ cup (60 mL) water; cook, stirring occasionally, for about 10 minutes or until it turns a dark caramel color. Carefully stir in ½ cup (125 mL) hot water (it will spatter). Stir in green onions, garlic, broth and fish sauce; cook, stirring, for 2 minutes to dissolve caramel. Season with ¼ tsp (1 mL) salt and pepper to taste. Press Cancel. Return ribs to pot.

4. Close and lock the lid and turn the steam release handle to Sealing. Set your Instant Pot to pressure cook on High for 20 minutes.

5. When the cooking time is done, press Cancel and let stand, covered, for 10 minutes, then turn the steam release handle to Venting. When the float valve drops down, remove the lid. The ribs should be fall-off-the-bone tender. (If more cooking time is needed, continue pressure cooking on High for 5 minutes, then quickly release the pressure.) Using tongs, transfer ribs to a deep platter and cover with foil.

6. Set your Instant Pot to sauté on Normal. Cook sauce, stirring, for 5 minutes or until it is thickened to your liking. Press Cancel. Season to taste with salt and pepper.

7. Drizzle about half the sauce over ribs. Serve extra sauce in a gravy boat.

TIP

You can substitute 1½ tsp (7 mL) soy sauce and ½ tsp (2 mL) miso paste for the fish sauce. The resulting flavor will not have quite as much umami, but it will still be wonderful.

CHICKEN

Almost Rotisserie Chicken

Why buy a rotisserie chicken at the grocery store when you can easily make almost rotisserie chicken at home? This delicately seasoned, moist, tender chicken can be served as is, or can be shredded and used in a variety of recipes. Or you can do a little bit of each.

MAKES ABOUT 4 SERVINGS OR ABOUT 3 CUPS (750 ML) SHREDDED CHICKEN

COOKING PROGRAMS

• Sauté •
• Pressure Cook •

• **Steam rack**

1	whole chicken (about 3 lbs/1.5 kg), trussed with wings and legs tied together (see tip), patted dry	1
1½ tbsp	poultry seasoning	22 mL
2 tsp	paprika	10 mL
1½ tsp	salt	7 mL
2 tbsp	butter	30 mL
1 tbsp	vegetable oil (approx.)	22 mL
¾ cup	ready-to-use chicken broth or Chicken Stock (page 27)	175 mL
1	bay leaf (optional)	1

1. Season chicken all over with poultry seasoning, paprika and salt. Set your Instant Pot to sauté on Normal. When the display says Hot, add butter and oil; heat until butter is melted. Add chicken and cook for about 8 minutes, turning often and adding more oil as necessary, until browned on all sides. Using tongs, transfer chicken to a plate.

2. Pour in broth and cook, scraping up any browned bits from the bottom of the pot, for about 1 minute. Add bay leaf (if using). Press Cancel.

3. Place the steam rack in the pot. Transfer chicken to the rack, breast side up. Add any accumulated juices from the chicken.

4. Close and lock the lid and turn the steam release handle to Sealing. Set your Instant Pot to pressure cook on High for 18 minutes.

5. When the cooking time is done, press Cancel and turn the steam release handle to Venting. When the float valve drops down, remove the lid. An instant-read thermometer inserted in the thickest part of the breast should register at least 165°F (74°C). (If more cooking time is needed, continue pressure cooking on High for 2 minutes.)

6. Transfer chicken to a cutting board, cover with foil and let rest for 10 minutes or until ready to carve or shred. Strain cooking liquid and make gravy (see tip), or let cool, cover and refrigerate for up to 3 days to use as stock (see tip).

TIPS

Measure the diameter of your inner pot and purchase a chicken that will fit in it.

If your chicken didn't come trussed, here's how to truss it: Cut a long piece of kitchen string (about 3 feet/90 cm). Place the chicken on a work surface, with the legs pointing away from you. Slide the middle of the string underneath the tail and back. Bring both ends up and over the legs, then crisscross the string between the legs and wrap it around the foot end. Pull the string tight until the legs are up and tight to the body. Pull the string down to the work surface and over the top of the wings. Flip the chicken over, pulling the string over the top. Wind the string three times around itself and, with the string under the neck, pull it very tight. Tie a knot in the string and cut off excess. Turn the chicken over, tuck the wing tips down behind the body and push the breast tip into the cavity. Your chicken should now be nice and compact.

TIPS

To make gravy, transfer the cooking liquid to a glass measuring cup and spoon off as much fat as possible. In a small bowl, stir together 1 tbsp (15 mL) all-purpose flour and 2 tbsp (30 mL) cold water to make a slurry. Stir slurry into cooking liquid until well combined. Set your Instant Pot to sauté on Less. When the display says Hot, add gravy and cook, stirring, for about 2 minutes or until thickened to your liking.

If using the leftover cooking liquid as stock, cover and refrigerate for up to 3 days. Skim fat from stock before using. You will have $2/3$ to 1 cup (150 to 250 mL) stock.

In place of poultry seasoning, you can use $1\frac{1}{2}$ tsp (7 mL) each dried sage, thyme and rosemary.

If your chicken came with giblets, you can add them to the pot in step 4.

Spicy Chicken with Chunky Tomatoes

Italian seasoning and hot pepper flakes take boring chicken breasts and turn them into a spicy and intriguing dish. Adding in tomatoes with onions and garlic transports you to an Italian countryside feast.

MAKES 4 SERVINGS

COOKING PROGRAMS
• Sauté • • Pressure Cook •

4	bone-in skin-on chicken breasts (about 1½ lbs/750 g total)	4
	Salt and freshly ground black pepper	
2 tbsp	virgin olive oil (approx.)	30 mL
¾ cup	ready-to-use reduced-sodium chicken broth or Low-Sodium Chicken Stock (variation, page 27)	175 mL
1 tbsp	dried Italian seasoning	15 mL
1 tsp	hot pepper flakes	5 mL
1	can (14 oz/398 mL) diced tomatoes with garlic and onion, with juice	1
2 tsp	chopped fresh basil (optional)	10 mL

1. Season chicken with salt and pepper. Set your Instant Pot to sauté on Normal. When the display says Hot, add 1 tbsp (15 mL) oil and heat until shimmering. Working in batches, add chicken, skin side down, and cook for 3 minutes or until skin is browned, adding more oil as needed between batches. Using tongs, transfer chicken to a plate as it is browned.

2. Add broth to the pot and cook, scraping up any browned bits from the bottom of the pot, for 1 minute. Press Cancel. Stir in Italian seasoning, hot pepper flakes and tomatoes with juice. Return chicken and any accumulated juices to the pot, arranging chicken skin side up.

3. Close and lock the lid and turn the steam release handle to Sealing. Set your Instant Pot to pressure cook on High for 12 minutes.

4. When the cooking time is done, press Cancel and turn the steam release handle to Venting. When the float valve drops down, remove the lid. An instant-read thermometer inserted in the thickest part of a breast should register 165°F (74°C) and the chicken should no longer be pink inside. (If more cooking time is needed, continue pressure cooking on High for 2 minutes.)

5. Using tongs, transfer chicken to serving plates. Spoon sauce over top. Serve garnished with basil, if desired.

TIPS

Do not use boneless skinless chicken breasts, as you will not get the intended results.

If you like your dishes spicier, you can add more hot pepper flakes after the chicken is done cooking. Pressure cooking intensifies the spiciness of hot pepper flakes.

Tender Chipotle Chicken

Fire up your taste buds with a spicy and smoky chipotle sauce that brings moist, tender chicken to new heights of deliciousness. This simple yet sensational dinner for two is done in a snap.

MAKES 2 SERVINGS

COOKING PROGRAMS

• Pressure Cook •
• Sauté •

½	chipotle chile pepper in adobo sauce	½
1	can (14½ oz/411 mL) fire-roasted tomatoes with garlic, with juice	1
¼ cup	packed fresh cilantro leaves	60 mL
	Water	
2	boneless skinless chicken breasts (each about 6 oz/175 g)	2
1 tbsp	cornstarch	15 mL
	Salt	

TIPS

If you like spicier chicken, you can increase the chipotle chile pepper to 1. (You may want to try the original amount first.)

You can substitute 2 chicken leg quarters for the breasts, if you prefer. Increase the cooking time in step 2 to 6 minutes.

When using the Quick Release method to release pressure, keep your hands and face away from the hole on top of the steam release handle so you don't get scalded by the escaping steam.

1. In the inner pot, combine chipotles, tomatoes with juice, cilantro and ½ cup (125 mL) water. Add chicken.

2. Close and lock the lid and turn the steam release handle to Sealing. Set your Instant Pot to pressure cook on High for 5 minutes.

3. When the cooking time is done, press Cancel and turn the steam release handle to Venting. When the float valve drops down, remove the lid. An instant-read thermometer inserted horizontally into the thickest part of a breast should register at least 165°F (74°C) and the chicken should no longer be pink inside. (If more cooking time is needed, close and lock the lid and let stand for 1 to 2 minutes.) Using tongs, transfer chicken to a plate and cover with foil to keep warm.

4. In a small bowl, whisk together cornstarch and 2 tbsp (30 mL) water.

5. Set your Instant Pot to sauté on Normal. Add cornstarch mixture and cook, stirring, for 4 to 6 minutes or until sauce is thickened. Press Cancel. Season to taste with salt.

6. Using tongs, return chicken to the pot and turn to coat with sauce. Transfer chicken to serving plates and serve with the remaining sauce.

SERVING SUGGESTION

Serve with a side of rice or a fresh green salad.

Roasted Pepper Stuffed Chicken Breast Rollups

These delicate chicken rollups are bursting with mozzarella, roasted peppers and basil, and an Italian seasoning blend adds just the right amount of flavor.

MAKES 4 SERVINGS

COOKING PROGRAM

• Pressure Cook •

- **8 wooden toothpicks**
- **Baking sheet, lined with heavy-duty foil**

4	boneless skinless chicken breasts (each about 6 oz/175 g)	4
1 tbsp	dried Italian seasoning, divided	15 mL
½ cup	shredded mozzarella cheese, divided	125 mL
¼ cup	chopped drained roasted red peppers, plus ¼ cup (60 mL) drained juice	60 mL
¼ cup	fresh basil chiffonade (see second tip, page 112)	60 mL
	Salt and freshly ground black pepper	
¾ cup	ready-to-use chicken broth or Chicken Stock (page 27)	175 mL

TIP

When using the Quick Release method to release pressure, keep your hands and face away from the hole on the top of the steam release handle so you don't get scalded by the escaping steam.

---

1. Place each chicken breast between two pieces of plastic wrap. Using a meat mallet or rolling pin, pound breasts to about ¼ inch (0.5 cm) thick. Remove plastic wrap. Sprinkle top of each breast evenly with ½ tsp (2 mL) Italian seasoning. Add 1 tbsp (15 mL) cheese to the center of each breast, leaving a ¾-inch (2 cm) border on all sides. Evenly divide roasted peppers and basil on top. Starting with a narrower end, roll breasts up and secure each with 2 toothpicks. Sprinkle tops with the remaining Italian seasoning. Season with salt and pepper.

2. Add roasted pepper juice and broth to the inner pot. Add chicken rollups.

3. Close and lock the lid and turn the steam release handle to Sealing. Press Pressure Cook and adjust the time to 4 minutes. Press Pressure Level until High is highlighted.

4. When the cooking time is done, press Cancel and turn the steam release handle to Venting. When the float valve drops down, remove the lid. The chicken should no longer be pink inside. (If more cooking time is needed, close and lock the lid and let stand for 2 minutes.)

5. Meanwhile, preheat broiler, with rack set 5 inches (12.5 cm) from the heat.

6. Transfer chicken rollups to prepared baking sheet and remove toothpicks. Sprinkle rollups with the remaining cheese, dividing evenly. Discard cooking liquid. Broil rollups for 1 to 2 minutes or until cheese is melted.

Tender Barbecue Chicken

Juicy, tender chicken slathered in your favorite barbecue sauce makes for an easy, delectable weeknight dinner for two — or for one, with leftovers for lunch. You can shred the leftover chicken and make a drool-worthy barbecue sandwich.

MAKES 2 SERVINGS

COOKING PROGRAMS

• Sauté •
• Pressure Cook •

4	bone-in skin-on chicken thighs (about 2 lbs/1 kg total)	4
1 tsp	paprika	5 mL
	Salt	
1 tbsp	virgin olive oil	15 mL
½	red onion, finely chopped	½
1	clove garlic, minced	1
1 cup	barbecue sauce (store-bought or see recipe, page 39)	250 mL
2 tbsp	water	30 mL

1. Sprinkle chicken with paprika and season with salt. Set your Instant Pot to sauté on Normal. When the display says Hot, add oil and heat until shimmering. Add chicken and cook, turning once, for 5 minutes or until browned on both sides. Using tongs, transfer chicken to a plate.

2. Add onion to the fat remaining in the pot and cook, stirring often, for 4 minutes or until softened. Add garlic and cook, stirring, for 1 minute or until fragrant. Press Cancel.

3. Stir in barbecue sauce and water. Return chicken and any accumulated juices to the pot, turning chicken to coat with sauce and finishing with the skin side up.

4. Close and lock the lid and turn the steam release handle to Sealing. Set your Instant Pot to pressure cook on High for 5 minutes.

5. When the cooking time is done, press Cancel and turn the steam release handle to Venting. When the float valve drops down, remove the lid. The juices should run clear when the chicken is pierced. (If more cooking time is needed, continue pressure cooking on High for 1 minute, then quickly release the pressure.)

6. Transfer chicken to a serving platter and spoon sauce over top.

SERVING SUGGESTION

To make sandwiches from any leftover chicken, remove and discard the skin. Using two forks, shred chicken and discard bones. Add chicken to a small saucepan, add more barbecue sauce to taste, if desired, and cook over medium heat until warmed through. Spoon chicken onto sandwich buns.

TIP

If the sauce is not the desired consistency at the end of step 5, transfer chicken to the platter, then set your Instant Pot to sauté on Normal. Simmer the sauce, stirring often, until it is thickened to your liking.

Moroccan Chicken

North African spices, citrus and honey add warm, inviting interest to seared chicken. You can skip the tagine and long cooking time while enjoying a surprising depth of flavor. Serve with carrots and a fruited couscous on the side.

MAKES 4 SERVINGS

COOKING PROGRAMS
• Sauté •
• Pressure Cook •

• **Steamer basket**

1½ tbsp	ras el hanout (see tips, page 59)	22 mL
4 tbsp	virgin olive oil, divided	60 mL
8	large bone-in skin-on chicken thighs (about 3 lbs/1.5 kg total)	8
	Salt	
1 cup	ready-to-use chicken broth or Chicken Stock (page 27)	250 mL
1 tbsp	liquid honey	15 mL
1 to 2 tbsp	freshly squeezed lemon juice, divided	15 to 30 mL
	Freshly ground black pepper	
2 tsp	sesame seeds	10 mL
	Lemon wedges (optional)	

1. In a large sealable plastic bag, combine ras el hanout and 3 tbsp (45 mL) oil. Add chicken, seal bag and toss lightly to evenly coat chicken. Arrange chicken in a single layer. Refrigerate for at least 1 hour or overnight.

2. Set your Instant Pot to sauté on Normal. Remove chicken from marinade, reserving marinade in bag. Season chicken lightly with salt. When the display says Hot, add chicken to the pot in batches and cook, turning once, for 5 minutes or until browned on both sides. Using tongs, transfer chicken to a plate as it is browned. Press Cancel.

3. Add marinade to the pot. Quickly add broth to bag and swish to rinse any remaining marinade, then pour into pot. Stir in honey and 1 tbsp (15 mL) lemon juice. Return chicken and any accumulated juices to the pot, turning chicken to coat with sauce and finishing with the skin side up.

4. Close and lock the lid and turn the steam release handle to Sealing. Set your Instant Pot to pressure cook on High for 5 minutes.

5. When the cooking time is done, press Cancel and turn the steam release handle to Venting. When the float valve drops down, remove the lid. The juices should run clear when the chicken is pierced. (If more cooking time is needed, continue pressure cooking on High for 1 minute.)

6. Transfer chicken to a serving platter. Season sauce to taste with more lemon juice, salt and pepper. Spoon sauce over chicken. Serve garnished with sesame seeds, with lemon wedges to squeeze over top, if desired.

Lemon Garlic Chicken and Asparagus

This easy, tender chicken dish gets a little sass from lemon juice and a bit of bite from garlic. Paired with delicate steamed asparagus, it creates a refreshing meal that won't weigh you down.

MAKES 2 SERVINGS

COOKING PROGRAMS

• Sauté •
• Pressure Cook •

• **Steamer basket**

4	cloves garlic, minced	4
½ tsp	salt	2 mL
⅛ tsp	freshly ground black pepper	0.5 mL
	Grated zest and juice of 1 lemon	
2 tbsp	virgin olive oil (approx.), divided	30 mL
4	bone-in skin-on chicken thighs (about 1½ lbs/750 g total)	4
1 cup	ready-to-use chicken broth or Chicken Stock (page 27)	250 mL
8 oz	asparagus spears, ends trimmed	250 g

1. In a large sealable plastic bag, combine garlic, salt, pepper, lemon zest, lemon juice and 1 tbsp (15 mL) oil. Add chicken to bag, seal and turn bag to coat chicken in marinade. Refrigerate for at least 1 hour or overnight.

2. Remove chicken from marinade, scraping any garlic and zest stuck on chicken back into the bag; reserve marinade.

3. Set your Instant Pot to sauté on Normal. When the display says Hot, add the remaining oil to the pot and heat until shimmering. Add chicken and cook, turning once, for 5 minutes or until browned on both sides. Press Cancel.

4. Add marinade to broth, stirring to combine. Pour over chicken.

5. Arrange asparagus in steamer basket and place on top of chicken.

6. Close and lock the lid and turn the steam release handle to Sealing. Set your Instant Pot to pressure cook on High for 4 minutes.

7. When the cooking time is done, press Cancel and turn the steam release handle to Venting. When the float valve drops down, remove the lid. Remove the steamer basket and set aside.

8. Close and lock the lid and turn the steam release handle to Sealing. Set your Instant Pot to pressure cook on High for 1 minute.

9. When the cooking time is done, press Cancel and turn the steam release handle to Venting. When the float valve drops down, remove the lid. The juices should run clear when the chicken is pierced. (If more cooking time is needed, continue pressure cooking on High for 1 minute.)

10. Transfer chicken to serving plates and drizzle with some of the liquid from the pot, discarding the remainder. Arrange asparagus around chicken.

SERVING SUGGESTION

Serve with Simple Rice Pilaf (page 33).

Valencia-Style Paella

The first time I ate paella, it was prepared by French and Spanish friends in northeastern France, near the German border. The second time was in a Cuban community in Florida. Both meals were outstanding, yet quite different, reflecting the diversity of this classic dish. This streamlined version reduces the traditionally long cooking time but still offers impeccable taste.

MAKES 6 SERVINGS

COOKING PROGRAMS

• Sauté •
• Pressure Cook •

2 tbsp	virgin olive oil (approx.)	30 mL
12 oz	smoked cured linguiça or chorizo sausage, cut into chunks	375 g
1 lb	boneless skinless chicken thighs, cut into 1-inch (2.5 cm) pieces	500 g
1	bag (16 oz/454 g) saffron yellow rice	1
2 cups	ready-to-use no-salt-added chicken broth or No-Salt-Added Chicken Stock (variation, page 27)	500 mL
2 cups	water	500 mL
½	jar (16 oz/473 mL) sliced roasted red peppers, drained	½
1 cup	frozen green peas	250 mL

TIP

If you cannot find a bag of saffron yellow rice, you can make your own by combining 2¼ cups (550 mL) long-grain white rice, 1 tbsp (15 mL) dried onion flakes, 1 tsp (5 mL) garlic powder, 1 tsp (5 mL) ground turmeric, ½ tsp (2 mL) salt and a pinch of saffron threads.

1. Set your Instant Pot to sauté on Normal. When the display says Hot, add oil and heat until shimmering. Add sausage and cook, stirring often, for 5 minutes or until slightly crispy. Using a slotted spoon, transfer sausage to a large bowl.

2. Working in batches, add chicken to the pot and cook, stirring, for 1 minute or until it turns white on all sides. Using a slotted spoon, add chicken to sausage as it is browned.

3. Add rice to the pot and cook, stirring, for 1 minute. Stir in broth and water; bring to a boil, scraping up any browned bits from the bottom of the pot. Return chicken, sausage and any accumulated juices to the pot. Stir in roasted peppers and peas. Press Cancel.

4. Close and lock the lid and turn the steam release handle to Sealing. Set your Instant Pot to pressure cook on High for 4 minutes.

5. When the cooking time is done, press Cancel and let stand, covered, for 10 minutes, then turn the steam release handle to Venting. When the float valve drops down, remove the lid. The juices should run clear when the chicken is pierced and the rice should be tender. (If more cooking time is needed, continue pressure cooking on High for 1 minute, then quickly release the pressure.)

Buffalo Chicken Wings

Chicken wings are always a hit at any party or game day celebration, and these classic Buffalo wings certainly fit the bill. The sheer simplicity of this recipe makes it a hit with the chef, too!

MAKES 6 SERVINGS AS AN APPETIZER

COOKING PROGRAMS
• Pressure Cook •
• Sauté •

- **Steamer basket**
- **Rimmed baking sheet, lined with foil, with a wire rack set on top**

¾ cup	Buffalo wing sauce	175 mL
¾ cup	barbecue sauce	175 mL
1 tbsp	Worcestershire sauce	15 mL
18	chicken wings, sections split apart, wing tips removed	18
	Blue cheese or ranch dressing	

1. In a large bowl, combine Buffalo sauce, barbecue sauce and Worcestershire sauce, stirring well. Add wings, tossing to fully coat in sauce.

2. Add 1 cup (250 mL) hot water to the inner pot and place the steamer basket in the pot (see tip). Arrange chicken wings in the steamer basket with as much of their surface exposed as possible. Set the remaining sauce aside.

3. Close and lock the lid and turn the steam release handle to Sealing. Set your Instant Pot to pressure cook on High for 6 minutes.

4. Meanwhile, preheat broiler, with rack set 4 inches (10 cm) from the heat.

5. When the cooking time is done, press Cancel and turn the steam release handle to Venting. When the float valve drops down, remove the lid. The juices should run clear when the chicken is pierced. (If more cooking time is needed, continue pressure cooking on High for 1 minute.) Using tongs, transfer wings to rack on prepared baking sheet. Pour out water and rinse inner pot.

6. Set your Instant Pot to sauté on Normal. Add the reserved sauce and cook, stirring often, for about 5 minutes or until thickened as desired.

7. Meanwhile, broil wings, turning once, for 3 to 4 minutes or until browned to your liking.

8. Transfer wings to a serving platter and drizzle or brush some of the sauce on top. Serve the remaining sauce and dressing on the side for dipping.

VARIATIONS

For spicier wings, increase the amount of Buffalo sauce and decrease the barbecue sauce by an equal amount.

For a sweeter flavor, use a honey barbecue sauce.

TIPS

This recipe makes 2 servings as a main course.

If your steamer basket doesn't have legs, place a steam rack in the pot first and place the steamer basket on the rack.

FISH AND SEAFOOD • FISH AND SEAFOOD • FISH AND SEAFOOD • FISH AND SEAFOOD • FISH AND SEAFOOD • FISH AND SEAFOOD • FISH AND SEAFOOD • FISH AND SEAFOOD • FISH AND SEAFOOD • FISH AND SEAFOOD • FISH AND SEAFOOD • FISH AND SEAFOOD • FISH AND SEAFOOD • FISH AND SEAFOOD • FISH AND SEAFOOD • FISH AND SEAFOOD • FISH AND SEAFOOD • FISH AND SEAFOOD • FISH AND SEAFOOD •

FISH AND SEAFOOD

Spicy Poached Cod

When you're tired of plain old fish fillets, try this recipe to take them up a notch. Herbs and spices add just the right amount of seasoning, while fresh lime juice adds cooling citrusy notes.

MAKES 2 SERVINGS

COOKING PROGRAM

• Pressure Cook •

- **Steam rack**
- **2 pieces parchment paper, cut to fit fillets**

1 cup	ready-to-use reduced-sodium chicken broth or Low-Sodium Chicken Stock (variation, page 27)	250 mL
12 oz	skinless cod fillet, cut into 2 equal pieces	375 g
	Virgin olive oil	
½ tsp	chili powder	2 mL
½ tsp	dried oregano	2 mL
¼ tsp	salt	1 mL
	Juice of ½ lime	
⅛ tsp	ground cumin	0.5 mL

TIP

Using your fingers, carefully check cod for tiny pin bones. Remove any bones with a tweezers or needle-nose pliers.

1. Add broth to the inner pot and place the steam rack in the pot. Brush cod on both sides with oil and place 1 piece, skin side down, on each prepared piece of parchment paper, tucking the thin end of the fish under to create an even thickness. Arrange both pieces on steam rack, without overlapping. Sprinkle cod with chili powder, oregano and salt.

2. Close and lock the lid and turn the steam release handle to Sealing. Set your Instant Pot to pressure cook on Low for 3 minutes.

3. When the cooking time is done, press Cancel and turn the steam release handle to Venting. When the float valve drops down, remove the lid. The fish should be opaque and should flake easily when tested with a fork. (If more cooking time is needed, continue pressure cooking on Low for 1 minute.)

4. Transfer fish to plates, squeeze lime juice over top and serve sprinkled with cumin.

SERVING SUGGESTION

Serve with a side of rice or steamed vegetables.

Delicate Lemon Pepper Flounder

Light, delicate flounder is infused with steaming onions from the bottom and tart lemon from the top. Refreshing cucumber completes this one-pot meal.

MAKES 2 SERVINGS

COOKING PROGRAM

• Pressure Cook •

- **Two 18- by 12-inch (45 by 30 cm) sheets parchment paper**
- **Steam rack**

½	small onion, thinly sliced and separated into rings	½
	Virgin olive oil	
	Salt and freshly ground black pepper	
2	skinless flounder fillets (each about 5 oz/150 g)	2
10	thin slices cucumber	10
6	thin slices lemon	6

TIPS

Haddock, sole, snapper or any thin lean light-meat fish with a delicate flavor can be used in place of the flounder.

Use the ⅛-inch (3 mm) setting on a mandoline (or a very sharp knife) to thinly slice the onion.

When quickly releasing pressure, remove the lid carefully, allowing steam to escape away from you.

---

1. Arrange onion rings in a line down the middle of each sheet of parchment paper. Drizzle with oil and season with salt and pepper. Place fish on top, drizzle with oil and season with salt and pepper. Arrange cucumber on top of fish and season with salt. Arrange lemon slices on top of cucumber. Fold parchment paper into tent-style packets (see page 13) and seal edges tightly.

2. Add 1 cup (250 mL) hot water to the inner pot and place the steam rack in the pot. Arrange packets on the rack, with room between them.

3. Close and lock the lid and turn the steam release handle to Sealing. Set your Instant Pot to pressure cook on Low for 6 minutes.

4. When the cooking time is done, press Cancel and turn the steam release handle to Venting. When the float valve drops down, remove the lid. Carefully open a packet. The fish should be opaque and should flake easily when tested with a fork. (If more cooking time is needed, reseal packet and continue pressure cooking on Low for 1 minute.)

5. Transfer packets to serving plates and cut open with scissors. Serve immediately.

Poached Tomato Basil Halibut

This aromatic dish pulls together tomatoes, basil and olives for a taste of the Mediterranean. While halibut is commonly used in this region, the dish can be made with a wide selection of white fish, depending upon availability and your preferences.

MAKES 2 SERVINGS

COOKING PROGRAM

• Pressure Cook •

- **4-cup (1 L) round heatproof dish, sprayed with nonstick cooking spray**
- **Steam rack**

3	tomatoes, thickly sliced, divided	3
10 oz	skinless halibut fillet, cut in half	300 g
3	cloves garlic, minced	3
1 tbsp	virgin olive oil	15 mL
	Salt and freshly ground black pepper	
3 tbsp	fresh basil chiffonade (see tip)	45 mL
1 tbsp	sliced drained kalamata olives	15 mL

TIPS

You can substitute tilapia, grouper, flounder, cod or sole for the halibut; decrease the pressure cooking time to 3 minutes.

To chiffonade basil, remove the stems and stack 10 or more leaves. Roll the leaves up lengthwise into a fairly tight spiral, then cut crosswise into thin strips. Fluff the strips.

1. Arrange half the tomatoes in prepared dish, overlapping as necessary. Carefully place fish in a single layer on top.

2. In a small bowl, combine garlic and oil. Brush top of fish with garlic oil. Season with salt and pepper. Top with basil. Arrange the remaining tomatoes on top.

3. Add 1½ cups (375 mL) hot water to the inner pot and place the steam rack in the pot. Place the dish on the rack.

4. Close and lock the lid and turn the steam release handle to Sealing. Set your Instant Pot to pressure cook on Low for 6 minutes.

5. When the cooking time is done, press Cancel and turn the steam release handle to Venting. When the float valve drops down, remove the lid. The fish should be opaque and should flake easily when tested with a fork. (If more cooking time is needed, close and lock the lid for 1 minute.)

6. Using a spatula, carefully transfer fish with tomatoes to serving plates. Serve garnished with olives.

Salmon with Sweet Mustard Sauce

Salmon gets a sweet and slightly pungent treatment with caramelized sugar paired with mustard and Worcestershire.

COOKING PROGRAMS

• Sauté •
• Pressure Cook •

- **6-cup (1.5 L) round heatproof dish**
- **Steam rack**

1 tbsp	packed brown sugar	15 mL
2 tsp	butter	10 mL
1 tbsp	virgin olive oil	15 mL
1 tbsp	Dijon mustard	15 mL
1 tbsp	Worcestershire sauce	15 mL
12 oz	skin-on salmon fillet, cut into 2 equal pieces	375 g

TIPS

Using your fingers, carefully check the salmon fillet for tiny pin bones. Remove any bones with a tweezers or needle-nose pliers.

When using the Quick Release method to release pressure, keep your hands and face away from the hole on top of the steam release handle so you don't get scalded by the escaping steam.

1. In the heatproof dish, combine brown sugar and butter.

2. Add 1 cup (250 mL) hot water to the inner pot and place the steam rack in the pot. Place a crisscross foil sling (see page 16) on the rack and place the dish in the sling. Set your Instant Pot to sauté on More. Stir mixture until sugar is melted and combined. Press Cancel.

3. Stir oil, mustard and soy sauce into sugar mixture, mixing well. Add salmon, turning to coat in sauce and arranging skin side down.

4. Close and lock the lid and turn the steam release handle to Sealing. Set your Instant Pot to pressure cook on Low for 5 minutes.

5. When the cooking time is done, press Cancel and turn the steam release handle to Venting. When the float valve drops down, remove the lid. The fish should be opaque and should flake easily when tested with a fork. (If more cooking time is needed, continue pressure cooking on Low for 1 minute.)

6. Using the foil sling, remove dish from the pot. Transfer salmon to serving plates and drizzle sauce over top. Serve immediately.

Herbed Salmon with Asparagus

This gourmet one-pot meal is one of my go-to dishes. The flavors are simple and pleasantly satisfying.

MAKES 2 SERVINGS

COOKING PROGRAMS

• Pressure Cook •
• Sauté •

- **Steam rack**
- **2 pieces of parchment paper, cut to fit salmon pieces**

1 cup	ready-to-use chicken broth or Chicken Stock (page 27)	250 mL
12 oz	skin-on salmon fillet, cut into 2 equal pieces	375 g
	Virgin olive oil	
	Herbes de Provence	
8 oz	asparagus spears, tough ends trimmed and spears halved	250 g
	Coarse salt and freshly ground black pepper	
3 tbsp	butter	45 mL
1 tbsp	freshly squeezed lemon juice	15 mL

TIP

Using your fingers, carefully check the salmon fillet for tiny pin bones. Remove any bones with a tweezers or needle-nose pliers.

---

1. Add broth to the inner pot and place the steam rack in the pot. Place 1 piece of salmon, skin side down, on each prepared piece of parchment paper and brush top with oil. Sprinkle with herbes de Provence. Arrange both pieces on steam rack, without overlapping. Arrange asparagus on top of salmon. Drizzle with a little oil and season with salt and pepper.

2. Close and lock the lid and turn the steam release handle to Sealing. Set your Instant Pot to pressure cook on Low for 5 minutes.

3. When the cooking time is done, press Cancel and turn the steam release handle to Venting. When the float valve drops down, remove the lid. The fish should be opaque and should flake easily when tested with a fork. (If more cooking time is needed, continue pressure cooking on Low for 1 minute.)

4. Transfer salmon to serving plates and arrange asparagus on top of and around salmon. Cover with foil to keep warm.

5. Set your Instant Pot to sauté on More. Cook, stirring often, for 3 minutes or until liquid is reduced to $1/4$ cup (60 mL). Add butter and lemon juice; cook, stirring, until butter is melted. Drizzle sauce over fish and asparagus. Serve immediately.

Tilapia with Corn and Peas

Preparing a meal in a paper packet — known as cooking *en papillote* — is a technique often used in fancier restaurants, but it works magically at home in your pressure cooker. Here, the subtle taste of tilapia is matched by the sweetness of corn and pea pods.

MAKES 2 SERVINGS

COOKING PROGRAM

• Pressure Cook •

- **Two 18- by 12-inch (45 by 30 cm) sheets parchment paper**
- **Steam rack**

1	lemon	1
¾ cup	frozen sweet corn kernels	175 mL
4 oz	sugar snap peas	125 g
2	skinless tilapia fillets (each about 5 oz/150 g)	2
1 tbsp	virgin olive oil	15 mL
1½ tsp	seafood seasoning (such as Old Bay)	7 mL
	Salt and freshly ground black pepper	

1. Grate lemon zest and measure 2 tsp (10 mL) zest. Juice enough of the lemon to measure 2 tbsp (30 mL) juice. Cut remaining lemon into wedges and set aside.

2. Arrange corn and peas in the center of each sheet of parchment paper, in a mound the size and shape of your tilapia fillet, dividing equally. Sprinkle with lemon zest. Place fish on top and drizzle with lemon juice and olive oil. Sprinkle with seafood seasoning. Season with salt and pepper. Fold parchment paper into tent-style packets (see page 13) and seal edges tightly.

3. Add 1½ cups (375 mL) hot water to the inner pot and place the steam rack in the pot. Arrange packets on the rack, with room between them.

4. Close and lock the lid and turn the steam release handle to Sealing. Set your Instant Pot to pressure cook on Low for 3 minutes.

5. When the cooking time is done, press Cancel and turn the steam release handle to Venting. When the float valve drops down, remove the lid. Carefully open a packet. The fish should be opaque and should flake easily when tested with a fork. (If more cooking time is needed, reseal packet and continue pressure cooking on Low for 1 minute.)

6. Transfer packets to serving plates and cut open with scissors. Serve immediately, with reserved lemon wedges to squeeze over top, if desired.

> **TIPS**
>
> You can substitute any thin (½-inch/ 1 cm thick or less) flaky white fish for the tilapia.
>
> If your Instant Pot doesn't have a Low pressure setting, cook on High for 1 minute.

Fish and Pineapple Tostadas

No need to travel down the Baja California peninsula when you can enjoy these sweet, spicy and tangy tostadas at home. Pineapple and hot pepper flakes work beautifully with the mild tilapia, and a tangy slaw crowns the dish.

MAKES 4 SERVINGS

COOKING PROGRAMS

- Sauté •
- Pressure Cook •

1 tbsp	vegetable oil (approx.)	15 mL
8	6-inch (15 cm) corn tortillas	8
	Salt	
1	can (20 oz/568 mL) pineapple chunks, with juice	1
½ tsp	hot pepper flakes	2 mL
¾ cup	water	175 mL
1½ lbs	skinless tilapia fillets, cut into large pieces	750 g
1 cup	deli-packed coleslaw	250 mL
1	avocado, cut into chunks (optional)	1

TIPS

You can substitute store-bought tostada shells for the tortillas and omit the oil and salt. Skip step 1. Before assembling the tostadas, heat the shells in the microwave on High for 10 to 20 seconds or until warmed.

If your Instant Pot doesn't have a Low pressure setting, cook on High for 1 minute.

1. Set your Instant Pot to sauté on Normal. When the display says Hot, add 1 tsp (5 mL) oil, turning pot to coat bottom, and heat until shimmering. Add 1 tortilla and cook, turning once, for 2 minutes or until lightly browned. Transfer to a plate lined with paper towel. Season with salt. Transfer drained tortilla to a foil sheet. Repeat with the remaining tortillas, adding more oil as necessary between tortillas and stacking drained tortillas on the foil. Wrap tortillas in foil to keep warm. Press Cancel.

2. Set aside 2 tbsp (30 mL) pineapple juice. Add pineapple and the remaining juice to the pot. Stir in hot pepper flakes and water. Add tilapia on top, overlapping as necessary; do not stir.

3. Close and lock the lid and turn the steam release handle to Sealing. Set your Instant Pot to pressure cook on Low for 3 minutes.

4. When the cooking time is done, press Cancel and turn the steam release handle to Venting. When the float valve drops down, remove the lid. The fish should be opaque and should flake easily when tested with a fork. (If more cooking time is needed, continue pressure cooking on Low for 1 minute.)

5. Meanwhile, stir reserved pineapple juice into coleslaw.

6. Layer 2 tortillas, mostly overlapping, on each serving plate. Using a slotted spoon, spoon fish and pineapple onto tortillas. Top with coleslaw. Serve garnished with avocado, if desired.

Steamed Mussels in Garlicky White Wine

Garlicky steamed mussels are great as an appetizer or for dinner. When you open the pot and smell the fabulous aromas of garlic, hot pepper and mussels, you will hardly be able to wait to start eating.

MAKES 2 SERVINGS AS A MAIN COURSE

COOKING PROGRAMS

• Sauté •
• Pressure Cook •

2 tbsp	virgin olive oil	30 mL
2	cloves garlic, minced	2
Pinch	hot pepper flakes	Pinch
2 lbs	mussels, scrubbed and debearded (see tip)	1 kg
1 cup	dry white wine or water	250 mL
1 cup	chopped fresh parsley	250 mL

TIPS

This dish serves 4 to 6 people as an appetizer.

To debeard mussels, grab the strands tightly and slide them out the side. Using a vegetable brush, scrub them under cold running water. Discard any cracked shells or shells that have already opened.

1. Set your Instant Pot to sauté on Normal. When the display says Hot, add oil and heat until shimmering. Add garlic and hot pepper flakes; cook, stirring, for 30 seconds. Add mussels and stir to coat. Stir in wine. Press Cancel.

2. Close and lock the lid and turn the steam release handle to Sealing. Set your Instant Pot to pressure cook on High for 1 minute.

3. When the cooking time is done, press Cancel and turn the steam release handle to Venting. When the float valve drops down, remove the lid. The mussels should be opened. (If more cooking time is needed, continue pressure cooking on High for 0 minutes.) Discard any mussels that do not open. Stir in parsley.

4. Ladle mussels and broth into serving bowls. Serve immediately.

Baked Stuffed Clams

These little mounds of deliciousness are often called "stuffies." They are little mounds of clams, spicy sausage, seasonings and bread cubes that are as wonderful to look at as they are to eat. Allow a couple of hours before the cooking time to soak the clams, to get rid of sand and grit.

MAKES 4 SERVINGS

COOKING PROGRAM

• Pressure Cook •

- **Steamer basket**
- **Food processor**
- **Rimmed baking sheet**

	Salt	
	Water	
8	large quahog clams (about 4 lbs/2 kg total)	8
6 oz	cooked andouille sausage, cut into 1½-inch (4 cm) pieces	175 g
3 cups	herb-seasoned cubed stuffing (see tips)	750 mL
¾ cup	chopped onion	175 mL
1¼ tsp	seafood seasoning (such as Old Bay)	6 mL
	Lemon wedges (optional)	

1. In a very large bowl, combine ⅓ cup (75 mL) salt and 8 cups (2 L) water, mixing well to dissolve salt. Add clams and let stand for 30 minutes. Drain clams. Repeat two or three times, until clams are purged.

2. Add 1 cup (250 mL) hot water to the inner pot and place the steamer basket in the pot (see tip). Arrange clams and sausage in basket.

3. Close and lock the lid and turn the steam release handle to Sealing. Set your Instant Pot to pressure cook on High for 5 minutes.

4. When the cooking time is done, press Cancel and turn the steam release handle to Venting. When the float valve drops down, remove the lid. The clams should be opened. (If more cooking time is needed, continue pressure cooking on High for 0 minutes.) Discard any clams that do not open. Reserve liquid in pot.

5. Preheat oven to 350°F (180°C).

6. Transfer clams to a work surface, open fully and remove meat. Reserve 12 half shells.

7. In food processor, process clams until finely chopped. Transfer to a large bowl.

8. Remove casings from sausage. In food processor, process sausage until finely chopped. Add to chopped clams.

9. Stir in stuffing, onion, seafood seasoning and ¾ cup (175 mL) reserved cooking liquid. Stir in additional liquid, 1 tbsp (15 mL) at a time, until desired moistness is reached.

10. Spoon crab mixture into shells and arrange on baking sheet.

11. Bake for 10 minutes or until stuffing is golden brown and mixture is heated through.

12. Transfer stuffed shells to serving plates and serve with lemon wedges, if desired.

TIPS

The large quahog clams used are also called chowders and are about 1 to 2 per lb (500 g). You can also use 12 cherrystone clams that are about 3 per lb (500 g). You do not need to change the cooking time for these.

Herb-seasoned stuffing cubes (such as Pepperidge Farm) are found in bags in the grocery store. If the packaged cubes are not available, you can use a crumb-like stuffing (such as Stove Top).

To make your own stuffing cubes for this recipe, cut 4 slices of herb-seasoned bread into ¾-inch (2 cm) cubes. Preheat oven to 275°F (140°C), with rack placed in the lower middle. Place cubes on a rimmed baking sheet and bake, stirring often, for about 50 minutes or until lightly browned and dry. Let cool to room temperature before use.

If your steamer basket doesn't have legs, place a steam rack in the pot first and place the steamer basket on the rack.

Stuffed clams can be frozen for up to 3 months. Skip step 5. After step 10, cover shells with plastic wrap and freeze until solid, then remove baking sheet from freezer, transfer clams to a resealable plastic bag and return to the freezer. Thaw overnight in the refrigerator before proceeding with steps 5 and 11. Increase the baking time to 12 minutes.

When removing the clams from the pot, lightly shake the steamer basket to drain off excess liquid.

Savory Crab Flan

This savory flan, which is similar to a crustless quiche, comes together easily, allowing you to prepare breakfast or lunch in a snap. The crab, green onions and seasoning meld perfectly, for an inviting, light and delicious meal.

MAKES 4 SERVINGS

COOKING PROGRAM

• Pressure Cook •

- **6-cup (1.5 L) round soufflé dish (7-inch/18 cm diameter), bottom lined with parchment paper**
- **Steam rack**

3	large eggs	3
2 tsp	seafood seasoning (such as Old Bay)	10 mL
Pinch	salt	Pinch
	Freshly ground black pepper	
1 cup	heavy or whipping (35%) cream	250 mL
1	can (6 oz/170 g) white crabmeat, drained (see tip)	1
¼ cup	thinly sliced green onions	60 mL

1. In a large bowl, whisk eggs. Whisk in seafood seasoning, salt, pepper to taste and cream. Stir in crab and green onions. Pour into prepared soufflé dish.

2. Add 1½ cups (375 mL) hot water to the inner pot and place the steam rack in the pot. Place a crisscross foil sling (see page 16) on the rack and place the soufflé dish in the sling.

3. Close and lock the lid and turn the steam release handle to Sealing. Set your Instant Pot to pressure cook on High for 12 minutes.

4. When the cooking time is done, press Cancel and let stand, covered, for 10 minutes, then turn the steam release handle to Venting. When the float valve drops down, remove the lid. A knife inserted in the center should come out clean. (If more cooking time is needed, continue pressure cooking on High for 2 minutes, then quickly release the pressure.)

5. Using the foil sling, carefully remove dish from the pot. Let stand for 10 minutes. Invert a plate on top of dish, then flip over to invert flan onto plate; peel off paper. Cut into 4 wedges and serve immediately.

SERVING SUGGESTION

Serve with steamed fresh asparagus or a crisp green salad for a mouthwatering pairing.

TIPS

When buying white crabmeat, make sure the can is 6 oz (170 g) net/total weight and 4 oz (120 g) drained weight.

For a spicier flavor, replace the black pepper with ⅛ tsp (0.5 mL) cayenne pepper.

You can replace the green onions with 1 tbsp (15 mL) snipped fresh chives.

Fiery Shrimp and Grits

Here, a traditional Southern dish is given a spicy intercontinental boost with harissa, a North African spice blend. Shrimp treated with this fiery mix of peppers are served atop creamy and cheesy grits, for a unique contrast of tastes.

MAKES 2 SERVINGS

COOKING PROGRAMS

• Pressure Cook •
• Sauté •

- **4-cup (1 L) heatproof bowl**
- **Steam rack**

1 tbsp	harissa paste (see tip)	15 mL
2 tsp	virgin olive oil	10 mL
	Salt	
8 oz	large shrimp (21/30 count), peeled, with tails intact, and deveined	250 g
½ cup	fine cornmeal	125 mL
	Water	
⅓ cup	shredded Parmesan cheese	75 mL
2 tbsp	butter	30 mL

1. In a medium bowl, combine harissa paste, oil and a pinch of salt. Add shrimp and toss to coat. Set aside.

2. In the heatproof bowl, combine cornmeal, ¼ tsp (1 mL) salt and 2 cups (500 mL) water, stirring well.

3. Add 1 cup (250 mL) hot water to the inner pot and place the steam rack in the pot. Place the heatproof bowl on the rack.

4. Close and lock the lid and turn the steam release handle to Sealing. Set your Instant Pot to pressure cook on High for 5 minutes.

5. When the cooking time is done, press Cancel and let stand, covered, for 10 minutes, then turn the steam release handle to Venting. When the float valve drops down, remove the lid. The cornmeal should be swollen and tender (see tip). (If more cooking time is needed, continue pressure cooking on High for 1 minute, then quickly release the pressure.)

6. Carefully remove bowl from the pot and add cheese and butter, whisking until blended and smooth. Set aside.

7. Empty water from pot and wipe dry. Set your Instant Pot to sauté on Normal. When the display says Hot, add shrimp and cook, turning occasionally, for 3 to 5 minutes or until pink, firm and opaque.

8. Ladle grits into serving bowls and top with shrimp and any oil from the pot. Serve immediately.

TIPS

Harissa paste varies widely in spiciness. Check the label and choose a paste that lists spices as the main ingredient, rather than onions and water. You can adjust the amount of paste if you want it less (or more!) spicy.

Cornmeal may be labeled "cornmeal," "polenta" or "grits." Do not use quick-cooking cornmeal.

Don't worry if the grits are too runny after step 5; they will thicken upon standing. If they are too firm after step 5, add water, 1 tbsp (15 mL) at a time, until they are your desired consistency.

BEANS, GRAINS AND PASTA • BEANS, GRAINS AND PASTA • BEANS, GRAINS AND PASTA • BEANS, GRAINS AND PASTA • BEANS, GRAINS AND PASTA • BEANS, GRAINS AND PASTA • BEANS, GRAINS AND PASTA • BEANS, GRAINS AND PASTA • BEANS, GRAINS AND PASTA • BEANS, GRAINS AND PASTA • BEANS, GRAINS AND PASTA • BEANS, GRAINS AND PASTA • BEANS, GRAINS AND PASTA • BEANS, GRAINS AND PASTA

BEANS, GRAINS AND PASTA

Make-and-Take Quinoa, Lentil and Cucumber Salad

Bring this protein-packed, refreshing salad to work for lunch, on a picnic or to a potluck. The cucumbers add a bright twist, and the vinaigrette pulls it all together.

MAKES 6 SERVINGS

COOKING PROGRAMS

• Sauté •
• Pressure Cook •

1½ tbsp	vegetable oil	22 mL
1 cup	quinoa, rinsed	250 mL
½ cup	dried green lentils, rinsed	125 mL
	Salt	
2¼ cups	water	550 mL
8 oz	grape tomatoes, quartered	250 g
1	cucumber, cut into ½-inch (1 cm) chunks	1
½ cup	Greek vinaigrette	125 mL
	Freshly ground black pepper	

TIP

The salad can be refrigerated in an airtight container for up to 2 days.

1. Set your Instant Pot to sauté on Normal. When the display says Hot, add oil and heat until shimmering. Add quinoa and cook, stirring, for 2 to 3 minutes or until lightly toasted. Press Cancel. Add lentils, ½ tsp (2 mL) salt and water, stirring well.

2. Close and lock the lid and turn the steam release handle to Sealing. Set your Instant Pot to pressure cook on High for 10 minutes.

3. When the cooking time is done, press Cancel and turn the steam release handle to Venting. When the float valve drops down, remove the lid. The quinoa and lentils should be tender, with a bit of texture. (If more cooking time is needed, close and lock the lid and let stand for 2 minutes.)

4. Transfer quinoa mixture to a fine-mesh sieve and rinse with cold water until chilled. Let drain for 10 minutes.

5. Meanwhile, add tomatoes and cucumbers to a colander set in a sink. Season with salt and toss lightly. Let drain in sink.

6. In a large bowl, combine quinoa mixture, tomatoes, cucumber and vinaigrette. Season to taste with salt and pepper. Serve immediately or, for optimum flavor, cover and refrigerate overnight.

Black Bean and Corn Salad

This refreshing salad combines beans, peppers, onions and corn for a multicolored presentation with the multidimensional flavors of the Southwest. It works well as a main course or side dish, or as an appetizer with tortilla chips for dipping.

MAKES 4 SERVINGS AS A MAIN COURSE

COOKING PROGRAM

• Pressure Cook •

2 cups	dried black beans	500 mL
	Water	
1 tbsp	vegetable oil (optional; see tip)	15 mL
2 cups	frozen corn kernels, thawed	500 mL
1	large bell pepper (any color), finely chopped	1
2 tbsp	chopped fresh cilantro	30 mL
¾ cup	lime vinaigrette	175 mL
	Salt and freshly ground black pepper	

TIPS

This salad serves 6 people as a side dish and 8 to 10 people as an appetizer.

Adding oil to the beans reduces the foaming that occurs with pressure cooking.

In place of the fresh bell pepper, you can substitute 1½ cups (375 mL) frozen mixed bell peppers and onions, thawed and finely chopped. These may also be labeled "pepper stir-fry."

1. In a large bowl, combine beans and 8 cups (2 L) cold water. Let stand at room temperature for 8 hours or overnight. Drain and rinse.

2. Add beans, 4 cups (1 L) fresh cold water and oil (if using) to the inner pot. Close and lock the lid and turn the steam release handle to Sealing. Set your Instant Pot to pressure cook on High for 2 minutes.

3. When the cooking time is done, press Cancel and let stand, covered, for 15 minutes, then turn the steam release handle to Venting. When the float valve drops down, remove the lid. The beans should be al dente. (If more cooking time is needed, continue pressure cooking on High for 1 minute, then quickly release the pressure.) Drain and rinse beans with cold water and let cool to room temperature.

4. In a large bowl, combine corn, pepper mixture, cilantro and vinaigrette. Add beans, mixing well. Let stand for 15 minutes to meld the flavors. Season to taste with salt and pepper.

Mediterranean Cannellini Salad

Transport yourself to the warm breezes of the Mediterranean with a light bean salad. So simple in its preparation, yet so complex in flavors and textures, this salad makes a wonderful summer lunch.

MAKES 3 TO 4 SERVINGS

COOKING PROGRAM

• Pressure Cook •

1 cup	dried cannellini (white kidney) beans	250 mL
	Water	
1 tbsp	virgin olive oil (optional; see tip)	15 mL
8 oz	grape tomatoes, quartered	250 g
⅔ cup	finely chopped fresh parsley	150 mL
¼ cup	Greek or Italian vinaigrette	60 mL
	Salt and freshly ground black pepper	
¼ cup	crumbled feta cheese	60 mL

TIP

Adding oil to the beans reduces the foaming that occurs with pressure cooking.

1. In a large bowl, combine beans and 4 cups (1 L) cold water. Let stand at room temperature for 8 hours or overnight. Drain and rinse.

2. Add beans, 2 cups (500 mL) fresh cold water and oil (if using) to the inner pot. Close and lock the lid and turn the steam release handle to Sealing. Set your Instant Pot to pressure cook on High for 5 minutes.

3. When the cooking time is done, press Cancel and let stand, covered, for 15 minutes, then turn the steam release handle to Venting. When the float valve drops down, remove the lid. The beans should be al dente. (If more cooking time is needed, continue pressure cooking on High for 1 minute, then quickly release the pressure.) Drain and rinse beans with cold water and let cool to room temperature.

4. In a large bowl, combine beans, tomatoes, parsley and vinaigrette, tossing gently. Season to taste with salt and pepper. Serve sprinkled with feta.

Cranberry Bean Salad with Tortellini and Pepperoncini

Pepperoncini adds a spicy hit to this hearty combination of beans and cheesy tortellini. This vegetarian delight is a perfect choice to pack for lunch.

MAKES 4 SERVINGS

COOKING PROGRAM

• Pressure Cook •

2 cups	dried borlotti (cranberry) beans, rinsed	500 mL
	Water	
1 tbsp	vegetable oil	15 mL
1	package (9 oz/255 g) fresh three-cheese tortellini pasta	1
9	pepperoncini peppers with brine	9
3 tbsp	chopped fresh parsley	45 mL
1/3 cup	extra virgin olive oil	75 mL
	Salt and freshly ground black pepper	
6 tbsp	shredded Parmesan cheese	90 mL

TIP

You can use a 7-oz (196 g) box of dried tortellini in place of fresh. In step 4, adjust the cooking time to half the time recommended on the box.

1. In a large bowl, combine beans and 8 cups (2 L) cold water. Let stand at room temperature for 8 hours or overnight. Drain and rinse.

2. Add beans, oil and 4 cups (1 L) fresh cold water to the inner pot. Close and lock the lid and turn the steam release handle to Sealing. Set your Instant Pot to pressure cook on High for 8 minutes.

3. When the cooking time is done, press Cancel and let stand, covered, for 15 minutes, then turn the steam release handle to Venting. When the float valve drops down, remove the lid. The beans should be al dente. (If more cooking time is needed, continue pressure cooking on High for 1 minute, then quickly release the pressure.) Drain and rinse beans with cold water and let cool to room temperature.

4. Set your Instant Pot to sauté on More. Add water according to pasta package directions and bring to a boil. Reduce heat to Normal. Add tortellini and cook according to package directions until al dente. Drain pasta, rinse with cold water and let cool to room temperature.

5. Meanwhile, drain peppers, reserving 1 1/2 tbsp (22 mL) brine. Slice peppers and set aside.

6. In a small bowl, whisk together parsley, oil and pepper brine. Season to taste with salt and pepper.

7. In a large bowl, combine beans, tortellini, peppers and dressing, tossing gently. Serve sprinkled with Parmesan.

Caprese-Style Chickpea Salad

I love a great Caprese salad. And I really, really love cucumbers. So why not use cucumbers to create this delightful riff on an Italian classic? Even better, it's powered up with hearty chickpeas, for a satisfying meal in a bowl.

MAKES 4 SERVINGS

COOKING PROGRAM

• Pressure Cook •

2 cups	dried chickpeas	500 mL
	Water	
1 lb	grape tomatoes, quartered	500 g
10 oz	fresh mozzarella balls (bocconcini), chopped	300 g
1	large cucumber, seeded and cut into ½-inch (1 cm) pieces	1
¾ cup	Italian or balsamic vinaigrette	175 mL
	Salt and freshly ground black pepper	

TIP

The salad can be prepared a day in advance. Cover and store in the refrigerator.

1. In a large bowl, combine chickpeas and 8 cups (2 L) cold water. Let stand at room temperature for 8 hours or overnight. Drain and rinse.

2. Add chickpeas and 4 cups (1 L) fresh cold water to the inner pot. Close and lock the lid and turn the steam release handle to Sealing. Set your Instant Pot to pressure cook on High for 10 minutes.

3. When the cooking time is done, press Cancel and let stand, covered, until the float valve drops down, then remove the lid. The chickpeas should be al dente. (If more cooking time is needed, continue pressure cooking on High for 1 minute, then quickly release the pressure.) Drain and rinse chickpeas with cold water and let cool to room temperature.

4. In a large bowl, combine chickpeas, tomatoes, mozzarella, cucumber and vinaigrette. Season to taste with salt and pepper. Let stand for 15 minutes before serving.

VARIATION

Add ½ cup (125 mL) chopped fresh basil just before serving for a fresh flavor boost.

Chickpea Coconut Curry

This easy vegetarian curry hits all the right notes. Packed with chickpeas, broccoli, cauliflower and carrots, and simmered in a coconut red curry sauce, it will tantalize your taste buds. Serve with Super-Simple Brown Rice (page 31) or Foolproof Jasmine Rice (page 32).

MAKES 4 SERVINGS

COOKING PROGRAMS

• Pressure Cook •
• Sauté •

- **Steamer basket**
- **2 rectangular sheets of heavy-duty foil**

1 cup	dried chickpeas	250 mL
	Water	
1	package (12 oz/340 g) fresh broccoli, cauliflower and carrot medley (see tip)	1
1 tbsp	vegetable oil	15 mL
	Salt and freshly ground black pepper	
1½ tsp	cornstarch	7 mL
1	can (14 oz/400 mL) coconut milk	1
2 tbsp	red curry paste	30 mL

1. In a large bowl, combine chickpeas and 4 cups (1 L) cold water. Let stand at room temperature for 8 hours or overnight (see tip). Drain and rinse.

2. Add chickpeas and 2 cups (500 mL) fresh cold water to the inner pot. Place the steamer basket on top (see fourth tip, page 119).

3. Divide vegetable medley evenly between foil sheets. Drizzle with oil. Season with salt and pepper. Fold foil into tent-style packets (see page 13) and seal edges tightly. Place packets in the basket.

4. Close and lock the lid and turn the steam release handle to Sealing. Set your Instant Pot to pressure cook on High for 10 minutes.

5. When the cooking time is done, press Cancel and let stand, covered, until the float valve drops down, then remove the lid. Transfer foil packets to a work surface and carefully open packets to release steam. Remove steamer basket. The chickpeas should be al dente. (If more cooking time is needed, continue pressure cooking on High for 1 minute, then quickly release the pressure.) Drain chickpeas.

6. In a small bowl, stir cornstarch into 2 tbsp (30 mL) cold water.

7. Set your Instant Pot to sauté on Normal. Add coconut milk and curry paste to the pot, mixing well. Stir in chickpeas. Add cornstarch mixture and cook, stirring, for 3 minutes or until thickened to your desired consistency. Stir in vegetable medley.

TIP

Packaged fresh vegetable medleys can be found in the produce section of the grocery store. Cut vegetables into 1-inch (2.5 cm) pieces, if necessary.

Wild West Pinto Beans

Pinto beans were enjoyed by wagon trains and wranglers throughout the Old West because they were easy to make and satisfying — and they still are today. You don't need to start a campfire for this plug-in-and-cook version.

MAKES 6 SERVINGS

COOKING PROGRAMS

- Sauté •
- Pressure Cook •

2 cups	dried pinto beans	500 mL
	Water	
2 tbsp	vegetable oil	30 mL
12 oz	slab side bacon	375 g
1	onion, cut into eighths	1
1	bay leaf (optional)	1
1 tbsp	paprika	15 mL
¼ tsp	cayenne pepper	1 mL
	Salt	

1. In a large bowl, combine beans and 8 cups (2 L) cold water. Let stand at room temperature for 8 hours or overnight. Drain and rinse.

2. Set your Instant Pot to sauté on Normal. When the display says Hot, add oil and heat until shimmering. Add bacon and cook, turning often, for 5 minutes or until browned on all sides. Using tongs, transfer bacon to a plate.

3. Add onion to the fat remaining in the pot and cook, stirring often, for 5 minutes or until lightly browned. Press Cancel. Return bacon to the pot. Add beans, 4 cups (1 L) fresh water and bay leaf (if using).

4. Close and lock the lid and turn the steam release handle to Sealing. Set your Instant Pot to pressure cook on High for 4 minutes.

5. When the cooking time is done, press Cancel and let stand, covered, for 15 minutes, then turn the steam release handle to Venting. When the float valve drops down, remove the lid. The beans should be al dente. (If more cooking time is needed, continue pressure cooking on High for 2 minutes, then quickly release the pressure.)

6. Stir in paprika and cayenne. Close and lock the lid and turn the steam release handle to Sealing. Set your Instant Pot to pressure cook on High for 5 minutes.

7. When the cooking time is done, press Cancel and let stand, covered, for 15 minutes, then turn the steam release handle to Venting. When the float valve drops down, remove the lid. Discard bay leaf (if using). Transfer bacon to a cutting board. Scoop out and discard about 1 cup (250 mL) of the cooking liquid. Using a potato masher, mash beans slightly.

8. Coarsely chop bacon and return to the pot. Set your Instant Pot to sauté on Normal. Season to taste with salt. Cook, stirring occasionally, for 5 minutes or until slightly thickened.

VARIATIONS

Vegetarian Wild West Beans: Omit the bacon and add 1 tbsp (15 mL) liquid smoke in step 3 with the water.

For a smokier flavor, use smoked paprika in place of regular.

Lemony Bulgur Tabbouleh

This riff on tabbouleh borrows ingredients from Lebanese cuisine — influences of lemon and loads of fresh parsley — while including more bulgur than a traditional Lebanese dish. This version is served hot, for another twist on the traditional. Cooking the bulgur in the Instant Pot makes it more tender than the usual method of soaking it in lemon juice and herbs.

MAKES 4 SERVINGS AS A MAIN COURSE

COOKING PROGRAM
• Pressure Cook •

- **4-cup (1 L) round casserole dish**
- **Steam rack**

1 cup	coarse bulgur, rinsed	250 mL
1½ cups	ready-to-use reduced-sodium vegetable broth or Low-Sodium Vegetable Stock (variation, page 28)	375 mL
2 tsp	virgin olive oil	10 mL
1 cup	chopped fresh parsley	250 mL
1 tsp	minced fresh oregano	5 mL
2 to 3 tbsp	freshly squeezed lemon juice	30 to 45 mL
	Salt and freshly ground black pepper	
8 oz	cherry tomatoes, quartered	250 g

1. In the casserole dish, combine bulgur, broth and oil. Add 1 cup (250 mL) hot water to the inner pot and place the steam rack in the pot. Place the dish on the rack.

2. Close and lock the lid and turn the steam release handle to Sealing. Set your Instant Pot to pressure cook on Low for 12 minutes.

3. When the cooking time is done, press Cancel and let stand, covered, for 5 minutes, then turn the steam release handle to Venting. When the float valve drops down, remove the lid. Using the handles of the rack, carefully remove dish from the pot and drain off any excess liquid from the dish.

4. Sprinkle parsley, oregano and 2 tbsp (30 mL) lemon juice over bulgur. Return rack and dish to the pot, close and lock the lid and let stand for 5 minutes.

5. Carefully remove dish from the pot and fluff bulgur gently with a fork, stirring in herbs. Season with salt and pepper. Taste and add more lemon juice as desired. Add tomatoes and toss gently to combine.

VARIATIONS

Three-Herb Bulgur Tabbouleh: Use ½ cup (125 mL) parsley and ½ cup (125 mL) chopped fresh basil. Substitute chopped fresh thyme for the oregano.

This dish can be chilled and served cold. You may want to toss in a coarsely chopped peeled cucumber before serving.

> **TIP**
> This tabbouleh serves 6 people as a side dish.

Quinoa-Stuffed Bell Peppers

Quinoa, tomatoes and taco seasoning mingle their textures and flavors as a filling for colorful bell peppers — a stunning presentation for a mouthwatering one-pot side dish or main course for two.

MAKES 2 SERVINGS AS A MAIN COURSE

COOKING PROGRAMS
• Sauté •
• Pressure Cook •

• **Steam rack**

3	large bell peppers (any color), divided	3
1 tbsp	virgin olive oil	15 mL
1	clove garlic, minced	1
⅔ cup	quinoa, rinsed	150 mL
3	plum (Roma) tomatoes, diced	3
2 tbsp	taco seasoning mix	30 mL
	Water	
	Salt and freshly ground black pepper (optional)	

1. Cut 2 of the bell peppers in half lengthwise and remove the stems, ribs and seeds; set aside. Finely chop the remaining pepper.

2. Set your Instant Pot to sauté on Normal. When the display says Hot, add oil and heat until shimmering. Add chopped pepper and cook, stirring often, for 3 to 5 minutes or until softened. Add garlic and cook, stirring, for 1 minute. Add quinoa and cook, stirring, for 1 minute or until lightly toasted. Stir in tomatoes, seasoning mix and 1 cup (250 mL) water. Press Cancel.

3. Close and lock the lid and turn the steam release handle to Sealing. Set your Instant Pot to pressure cook on High for 2 minutes.

4. When the cooking time is done, press Cancel and let stand, covered, for 10 minutes, then turn the steam release handle to Venting. When the float valve drops down, remove the lid.

5. If desired, season quinoa mixture to taste with salt and pepper. Spoon into bell pepper halves, packing well and mounding on top as needed. Wash and dry the pot and return to the cooker.

6. Add 1 cup (250 mL) hot water to the pot and place the steam rack in the pot. Arrange the filled peppers on the rack, stacking one in the center of the others as needed.

7. Close and lock the lid and turn the steam release handle to Sealing. Set your Instant Pot to pressure cook on High for 7 minutes.

8. When the cooking time is done, press Cancel and turn the steam release handle to Venting. When the float valve drops down, remove the lid. The peppers should be softened to your liking. (If more cooking time is needed, continue pressure cooking on High for 1 minute.)

9. Using silicone-coated tongs, transfer peppers to individual serving plates. Serve immediately.

SERVING SUGGESTION

Serve topped with sliced black olives, chopped avocado, sliced green onions and/or sliced pickled jalapeño peppers.

TIPS

This dish serves 4 people as a side dish.

Using silicone-coated tongs to remove the peppers from the pressure cooker will help you avoid poking through the skin of the peppers. If you don't have them, just use regular tongs.

If using canned diced tomatoes in place of fresh, you will need 1 cup (250 mL) drained.

Simply Perfect Risotto with Peas

Risotto may seem fussy and complicated, but in the Instant Pot it is really quite simple, and the results are delightful every time. Once you have perfected this dish, you will find yourself serving it all the time, to accompany just about anything.

MAKES 6 SERVINGS

COOKING PROGRAMS

• Sauté •
• Pressure Cook •

¼ cup	butter, softened, divided	60 mL
1	leek (white and light green parts only), thinly sliced	1
2 cups	Arborio rice	500 mL
4 cups	ready-to-use reduced-sodium vegetable or chicken broth, Low-Sodium Vegetable Stock (variation, page 28) or Low-Sodium Chicken Stock (variation, page 27)	1 L
1 cup	hot water (approx.)	250 mL
	Salt	
1 cup	frozen sweet peas, thawed	250 mL
½ cup	freshly grated Parmesan cheese	125 mL
	Freshly ground black pepper	

TIPS

Do not substitute another type of rice in this recipe. Arborio rice gives the dish the right amount of texture and starch for a perfect risotto.

If the risotto is runnier after step 3 than you prefer, let it stand, uncovered, stirring occasionally, for 2 minutes, then continue with step 4.

1. Set your Instant Pot to sauté on Normal. When the display says Hot, add 2 tbsp (30 mL) butter and heat until melted. Add leek and cook, stirring, for 2 to 3 minutes or until softened. Add rice, stirring to coat with butter. Press Cancel. Stir in broth, hot water and ¼ tsp (1 mL) salt.

2. Close and lock the lid and turn the steam release handle to Sealing. Set your Instant Pot to pressure cook on High for 4 minutes.

3. When the cooking time is done, press Cancel and turn the steam release handle to Venting. When the float valve drops down, remove the lid. The rice should be al dente. (If more cooking time is needed, continue pressure cooking on High for 1 minute.)

4. Set your Instant Pot to sauté on Normal. Gently stir in peas, Parmesan and the remaining butter; cook, stirring and adding more hot water or broth, if desired, for 1 to 3 minutes or until rice is done to your liking. Season to taste with salt and pepper. Serve immediately.

Garam Masala Basmati Rice

A common ingredient in Indian cooking, garam masala adds warm and spicy seasoning to this versatile rice dish. Serve it with curries, dals and gravies for an Indian-inspired meal.

MAKES 4 SERVINGS

COOKING PROGRAMS

• Sauté •
• Pressure Cook •

1 cup	basmati rice	250 mL
	Cold water	
2 tbsp	vegetable oil	30 mL
¼ cup	raw cashews, coarsely chopped	60 mL
2 tbsp	butter or ghee	30 mL
1	onion, chopped	1
1	clove garlic, minced	1
1 tsp	garam masala	5 mL
1 cup	ready-to-use vegetable broth or Vegetable Stock (page 28)	250 mL

TIPS

Basmati rice is a variety of rice that requires soaking, which enables a flavor compound in the rice to come to its full potential. Rinsing the rice removes excess starch to prevent sticky rice.

Garam masala is an Indian seasoning blend. Look for it in the spice section of well-stocked grocery stores.

1. Place rice in a medium bowl and cover with cold water; let stand for 30 minutes. Drain and rinse.

2. Set your Instant Pot to sauté on Normal. When the display says Hot, add oil and heat until shimmering. Add cashews and cook, stirring, for 2 minutes or until lightly toasted. Using a slotted spoon, transfer cashews to a plate lined with paper towel.

3. Add butter to the pot and heat until melted. Add onion and cook, stirring often, for 3 minutes or until translucent. Add garlic and garam masala; cook, stirring, for 1 minute or until fragrant. Add rice and cook, stirring, until well coated. Stir in broth. Press Cancel.

4. Close and lock the lid and turn the steam release handle to Sealing. Set your Instant Pot to pressure cook on High for 1 minute.

5. When the cooking time is done, press Cancel and let stand, covered, for 10 minutes, then turn the steam release handle to Venting. When the float valve drops down, remove the lid. The rice should be tender. (If more cooking time is needed, close and lock the lid and let stand for 3 minutes.)

6. Fluff rice with a fork. Serve immediately, sprinkled with cashews.

Wild and Brown Rice Medley

The hearty texture and depth of flavor in this versatile side dish make it the ideal accompaniment to chicken, pork or lamb.

MAKES 8 SERVINGS

COOKING PROGRAMS

• Sauté •
• Pressure Cook •

2 tbsp	butter	30 mL
1	onion, finely chopped	1
2 cups	sliced mushrooms	500 mL
2	cloves garlic, minced	2
2 cups	long-grain brown and wild rice blend	500 mL
2 tsp	finely chopped fresh thyme	10 mL
2½ cups	ready-to-use vegetable broth or Vegetable Stock (page 28)	625 mL
	Salt and freshly ground black pepper	

TIPS

Make sure your rice blend uses long-grain brown rice and not brown basmati rice, which may not work with the same cooking time.

If using dried thyme in place of fresh, reduce the amount to ¾ tsp (3 mL).

If the rice is crunchy at the end of the 20-minute cooking time, you may need to add 1 to 2 tbsp (15 to 30 mL) water before continuing to cook, to prevent the rice from sticking to the bottom of the pot.

1. Set your Instant Pot to sauté on Normal. When the display says Hot, add butter and heat until melted. Add onion and mushrooms; cook, stirring often, for 5 to 7 minutes or until mushrooms have released most of their moisture and onion is softened. Add garlic and cook, stirring, for 1 minute. Add rice mixture and cook, stirring, for 2 minutes or until lightly toasted. Stir in thyme and broth, scraping up any browned bits from the bottom of the pot. Press Cancel.

2. Close and lock the lid and turn the steam release handle to Sealing. Set your Instant Pot to pressure cook on High for 20 minutes.

3. When the cooking time is done, press Cancel and let stand, covered, until the float valve drops down, then remove the lid. The rice should be tender. (If more cooking time is required, continue pressure cooking on High for 2 minutes, then quickly release the pressure.)

4. Fluff rice with a fork. Season to taste with salt and pepper. Serve immediately.

Simply Sensational Lasagna

I can't decide what I love more about this lasagna: how fast and simple it is to make, or how sensational it tastes. For all these reasons, it has become a staple in my kitchen. I especially love it topped with grated Parmesan.

MAKES 4 TO 6 SERVINGS

COOKING PROGRAM
• Pressure Cook •

- **6-inch (15 cm) springform pan (about 3 inches/7.5 cm deep), sprayed with nonstick cooking spray (see tip)**
- **Steam rack**

1	jar (24 oz/682 mL) pasta sauce with Italian sausage, peppers and onions, divided	1
¼ cup	water	60 mL
1	large egg	1
2½ cups	shredded Italian cheese blend, divided	625 mL
1 cup	ricotta cheese	250 mL
6 oz	oven-ready (no-boil) lasagna noodles	175 g

1. Add ½ inch (1 cm) sauce to prepared baking pan. Transfer remaining sauce to a bowl and stir in water.

2. In a large bowl, whisk egg. Stir in 1¾ cups (425 mL) Italian cheese blend and ricotta.

3. Layer one-quarter of the noodles on top of sauce in pan, breaking noodles as needed to evenly cover sauce. Top with one-third of the cheese mixture, then one-quarter of the sauce. Continue with two more layers each of noodles, cheese mixture and sauce, gently pressing down on the noodles between each layer. Finish with a layer of noodles and a layer of sauce (the pan will be very full).

4. Add 1½ cups (375 mL) water and the steam rack to the pot. Place the baking pan on the rack.

5. Close and lock the lid and turn the steam release handle to Sealing. Set your Instant Pot to pressure cook on High for 14 minutes.

6. When the cooking time is done, press Cancel and turn the steam release handle to Venting. When the float valve drops down, remove the lid. Sprinkle with the remaining Italian cheese blend. Close and lock the lid and let stand for 10 minutes or until cheese is melted.

7. Using the handles of the rack, carefully remove the rack and pan. Let lasagna stand for 10 minutes (to make it easier to cut). Cut into wedges.

TIPS

You can line the bottom of the springform pan with parchment paper and let the paper stick out from the bottom ring of the pan as you are clamping it shut. This will prevent any sauce from leaking into the bottom of the pot.

You can use any flavor of pasta sauce you prefer or try Instant Marinara Sauce (page 36).

Butterfly Pasta Carbonara

This variation of a traditional carbonara uses farfalle pasta instead of linguine. Not only does it look like tiny little butterflies, but it has more nooks and crannies for the decadent sauce to cling to, making every bite a bit of splendor.

MAKES 8 SERVINGS

COOKING PROGRAMS

• Sauté •
• Pressure Cook •

1½ tbsp	virgin olive oil	22 mL
5 oz	slab pancetta or side bacon, cut into ¼-inch (0.5 cm) cubes	150 g
1 lb	dried farfalle pasta	500 g
	Salt	
7 cups	water	1.75 L
5	large eggs, at room temperature	5
1 cup	freshly grated Parmesan cheese	250 mL
	Freshly ground black pepper	
	Additional freshly grated Parmesan cheese (optional)	

1. Set your Instant Pot to sauté on Normal. When the display says Hot, add oil and heat until shimmering. Add pancetta and cook, stirring, for 3 to 5 minutes or until fat is rendered but not yet crispy on the edges. Press Cancel. Using a slotted spoon, transfer pancetta to a plate. Discard all but 1 tbsp (15 mL) fat from the pot.

2. Add pasta, ¼ tsp (1 mL) salt and water to the pot. Close and lock the lid and turn the steam release handle to Sealing. Set your Instant Pot to pressure cook on High and adjust the time to half the time recommended on the pasta package minus 1 minute. (If the cooking time is a range, use half of the higher number minus 1 minute.)

3. When the cooking time is done, press Cancel and turn the steam release handle to Venting. When the float valve drops down, remove the lid. The pasta should be slightly more tender than al dente. (If more cooking time is needed, continue pressure cooking on High for 1 minute.) Drain pasta, reserving 1 cup (250 mL) pasta water.

4. Meanwhile, separate 2 of the eggs and save the whites for another use (see tip). In a medium bowl, whisk together 3 eggs, 2 egg yolks and Parmesan. Season with salt and pepper.

5. Return pasta and pancetta to the pot. Set your Instant Pot to sauté on Less. Cook, stirring gently, for 2 minutes or until warmed through. Press Cancel. Quickly stir in egg mixture until creamy, adding reserved pasta water, 2 tbsp (30 mL) at a time, if needed for creaminess. Season to taste with pepper. Serve garnished with additional Parmesan cheese, if desired.

TIPS

Use long tongs or a long spoon when cooking pancetta, as the hot oil may splatter and burn.

The eggs in this recipe are only lightly cooked. For optimal food safety, use pasteurized in-shell eggs if they are available in your area.

Leftover egg whites can be stored in an airtight container in the freezer for up to 3 months. Use them to make meringues and other desserts.

My-Oh-My Mac 'n' Cheese

Some evenings you just want to curl up with a childhood favorite comfort food. What seems to satisfy that urge best is cheesy, creamy macaroni and cheese. My oh my, how we love our mac 'n' cheese!

MAKES 4 SERVINGS

COOKING PROGRAMS

• Pressure Cook •
• Sauté •

2 cups	dried elbow macaroni	500 mL
	Salt	
2 cups	ready-to-use reduced-sodium chicken or vegetable broth, Low-Sodium Chicken Stock (variation, page 27) or Low-Sodium Vegetable Stock (variation, page 28)	500 mL
1	can (12 oz or 370 mL) evaporated milk	1
2½ cups	shredded Cheddar cheese	625 mL
	Freshly ground black pepper	

TIPS

Two cups (500 mL) elbow macaroni is about 8 oz (250 g).

You can double this recipe, provided you do not fill your Instant Pot above the maximum fill line.

When using the Quick Release method to release pressure, keep your hands and face away from the hole on top of the steam release handle so you don't get scalded by the escaping steam.

1. In the inner pot, combine macaroni, ¼ tsp (1 mL) salt and broth. Close and lock the lid and turn the steam release handle to Sealing. Set your Instant Pot to pressure cook on Low for 3 minutes.

2. When the cooking time is done, press Cancel and turn the steam release handle to Venting. When the float valve drops down, remove the lid. The pasta should be al dente. (If more cooking time is necessary, close and lock the lid and let stand for 1 minute.)

3. Stir in milk. Set your Instant Pot to sauté on Less. Cook, stirring, for 2 to 3 minutes or until sauce has thickened and pasta is done to your liking. Press Cancel. Add cheese, ½ cup (125 mL) at a time, stirring until melted and combined before adding more. Season to taste with salt and pepper. Serve immediately.

VARIATION

Zesty Mac 'n' Cheese: In step 1, stir in 1 tsp (5 mL) dry mustard and ¼ tsp (1 mL) cayenne pepper with the salt.

VEGETABLES AND SIDES

Roman-Style Artichokes

Have you ever looked at those beautifully colored, flower bud–shaped vegetables in the produce section and wondered just how to prepare them? This classic Italian dish with just a little prep work will make the buttery, melt-in-your-mouth gems a vegetable you won't pass up again.

MAKES 2 TO 4 SERVINGS

COOKING PROGRAM

• Pressure Cook •

• **Steamer basket**

	Water	
	Juice of 1 lemon	
4	medium artichokes	4
½ cup	loosely packed fresh parsley leaves, finely chopped	125 mL
¼ cup	loosely packed fresh mint leaves, finely chopped	60 mL
3	cloves garlic, minced	3
3 tbsp	virgin olive oil	45 mL
	Salt and freshly ground black pepper	
1	lemon, cut into wedges	1

1. Fill a large bowl with water and lemon juice. Trim artichokes (see tip) and add to the lemon water.

2. Add 1 cup (250 mL) hot water to the inner pot and place the steamer basket in the pot (see tip).

3. In a small bowl, combine parsley, mint, garlic and oil, mixing well. Set aside about one-quarter of the herb mixture.

4. Remove artichokes from lemon water and stuff the centers with the remaining herb mixture, dividing evenly. Arrange artichokes, stem side up, in the basket, allowing room around each artichoke for steam to move.

5. Close and lock the lid and turn the steam release handle to Sealing. Set your Instant Pot to pressure cook on High for 12 minutes.

6. When the cooking time is done, press Cancel and let stand, covered, for 10 minutes, then turn the steam release handle to Venting. When the float valve drops down, remove the lid. The artichoke centers should be fork-tender. (If more cooking time is needed, continue pressure cooking on High for 2 minutes, then quickly release the pressure.)

7. Using a spoon, transfer artichokes, stem side down, to serving plates and sprinkle with the reserved herb mixture. Season to taste with salt and pepper. Serve warm or at room temperature, with lemon wedges on the side to squeeze over top.

VARIATION

Replace $\frac{1}{2}$ cup (125 mL) of the water in step 2 with a dry white wine, such as Pinot Grigio, if you prefer. White wine interacts with the artichokes to give them a slightly sweeter taste.

TIPS

To trim artichokes, begin by cutting the stems to within $\frac{1}{2}$ inch (1 cm) of the base. Cut off the hard, darker leaves near the base. Periodically dip the artichokes in the lemon water to prevent browning. Slice off the top of each artichoke, about halfway down, until you see the tender leaves around the choke. Using your fingers, peel off the tougher outer leaves. Using a small spoon, open up the inner leaves, carve out the hairy choke and discard. Leave artichokes in lemon water until ready to use.

If your steamer basket doesn't have legs, place a steam rack in the pot first and place the steamer basket on the rack.

Tangy Brussels Sprouts with Bacon

When prepared correctly, Brussels sprouts transform into a scrumptious side dish that will please even those who were adamant they would never eat them again.

COOKING PROGRAMS

• Sauté •
• Pressure Cook •

	Nonstick cooking spray	
4	slices thick-cut bacon, finely chopped	4
1	large shallot, thinly sliced	1
3	cloves garlic, minced	3
1 cup	ready-to-use reduced-sodium chicken broth or Low-Sodium Chicken Stock (variation, page 27)	250 mL
1 lb	Brussels sprouts, trimmed and cut in half	500 g
½ tsp	salt	2 mL
¼ tsp	freshly ground black pepper	1 mL
1 tbsp	balsamic vinegar reduction (see tip)	15 mL

1. Spray the bottom of the inner pot with cooking spray. Set your Instant Pot to sauté on Normal. When the display says Hot, add bacon and cook, stirring, for 4 to 5 minutes or until medium-crisp. Using a slotted spoon, transfer bacon to a plate lined with paper towel.

2. Add shallot to the fat remaining in the pot and cook, stirring, for 3 minutes or until softened. Add garlic and cook, stirring, for 1 minute or until fragrant. Add broth and scrape up any browned bits from the bottom of the pot. Press Cancel. Stir in Brussels sprouts, salt, pepper and vinegar reduction.

3. Close and lock the lid and turn the steam release handle to Sealing. Set your Instant Pot to pressure cook on High for 2 minutes.

4. When the cooking time is done, press Cancel and turn the steam release handle to Venting. When the float valve drops down, remove the lid. A fork inserted in the stem end of a sprout should pierce it easily. (If more cooking time is needed, close and lock the lid and let stand for 2 minutes.)

5. Transfer sprout mixture to a serving bowl and sprinkle with bacon.

TIPS

Choose Brussels sprouts that are uniform in size, for even cooking.

You can purchase balsamic vinegar reduction or make your own. In a small saucepan, bring 1 cup (250 mL) balsamic vinegar and ¼ cup (60 mL) liquid honey or pure maple syrup to a boil over high heat. Reduce heat and simmer for 10 minutes or until reduced to about ⅓ cup (75 mL). Let cool. Leftover balsamic vinegar reduction can be drizzled over a caprese salad, cut fruits or roasted vegetables.

Valencia-Style
Paella (page 106)

Buffalo Chicken Wings (page 107)

Herbed Salmon with Asparagus (page 114)
and Simple Rice Pilaf (page 33)

Fish and Pineapple Tostadas (page 116)

Baked Stuffed Clams (page 118)

Cranberry Bean Salad with Tortellini
and Pepperoncini (page 127)

Simply Sensational Lasagna (page 137)

Lip-Smacking Peach Cobbler (page 175)

Beets with Dijon Vinaigrette and Chèvre

Steaming whole beets under pressure keeps them moist, concentrates their flavor and reduces bleeding. A classic Dijon vinaigrette highlights their flavor even more, and the salty chèvre completes the balance.

| MAKES 6 SERVINGS |

COOKING PROGRAM

• Pressure Cook •

• **Steamer basket**

8	small red beets (about 2 lbs/ 1 kg total)	8
	Ice water	
2½ tbsp	white wine vinegar	37 mL
1¼ tsp	Dijon mustard	6 mL
	Salt	
⅓ cup	extra virgin olive oil	75 mL
	Freshly ground black pepper	
¼ cup	crumbled chèvre	60 mL
	Chopped walnuts (optional)	

TIPS

When handling beets, you may want to wear kitchen gloves so you don't discolor your hands. Wash any utensils and work surfaces immediately to avoid discoloration.

Beet greens can be discarded or saved for another use.

You can prepare the beets through step 4 up to 2 days ahead. Transfer beets to a bowl of ice water and let cool. Drain beets, but do not peel. Cover tightly and refrigerate. When ready to serve, continue with step 5, beginning with peeling the beets.

1. Cut greens from beets, leaving 1 inch (2.5 cm) stem on. Do not cut root end. Scrub beets well.

2. Add 1 cup (250 mL) hot water to the inner pot and place the steamer basket in the pot (see third tip, page 147). Arrange beets in the basket.

3. Close and lock the lid and turn the steam release handle to Sealing. Set your Instant Pot to pressure cook on High for 18 minutes.

4. When the cooking time is done, press Cancel and turn the steam release handle to Venting. When the float valve drops down, remove the lid. The beets should be fork-tender. (If more cooking time is needed, continue pressure cooking on High for 2 minutes.)

5. Transfer beets to a bowl of ice water and let cool. Peel beets and discard skins. Cut each beet into 6 wedges and transfer to a serving plate.

6. In a small bowl, whisk together vinegar, mustard and ¼ tsp (1 mL) salt. Gradually whisk in oil. Season to taste with salt and pepper.

7. Drizzle beets with vinaigrette and toss gently to coat. Sprinkle with chèvre. Serve garnished with walnuts, if desired.

VARIATIONS

Tarragon Vinaigrette: Replace the Dijon mustard with 1 tbsp (15 mL) minced fresh tarragon.

Garlic Vinaigrette: Replace the Dijon mustard with 2 tsp (10 mL) minced garlic.

Wilted Beet Greens

Beet greens have a wonderful array of nutrients, and you can either purchase them as-is or use leftover greens from trimming beets. Here, they get amped up with garlic and hot pepper flakes, but you'll also want to try the simple and delicious variations.

MAKES 3 SERVINGS

COOKING PROGRAMS

• Pressure Cook •
• Sauté •

• **Steamer basket**

	Salt	
1 lb	beet greens (see tips)	500 g
1½ tbsp	virgin olive oil	22 mL
2	cloves garlic, minced	2
¼ tsp	hot pepper flakes	1 mL
	Freshly ground black pepper	

1. Add 1 cup (250 mL) hot water and 1 tbsp (15 mL) salt to the inner pot and place the steamer basket in the pot (see tip). Arrange beet greens in the basket.

2. Close and lock the lid and turn the steam release handle to Sealing. Set your Instant Pot to pressure cook on High for 3 minutes.

3. When the cooking time is done, press Cancel and turn the steam release handle to Venting. When the float valve drops down, remove the lid. The beet greens should be wilted. (If more cooking time is necessary, close and lock the lid and let stand for 1 minute.)

4. Transfer beet greens to a cutting board and coarsely chop. Rinse and dry the pot and return to the cooker.

5. Set your Instant Pot to sauté on Normal. When the display says Hot, add oil and heat until shimmering. Add garlic and hot pepper flakes; cook, stirring, for 1 minute or until fragrant. Add greens and cook, stirring, for 2 minutes or until greens are well combined with garlic and oil.

6. Transfer greens to a serving plate and season to taste with salt and pepper.

SERVING SUGGESTION

For a main course, add 1½ cups (375 mL) cooked quinoa (see Quick and Easy Quinoa, page 30) and 2 medium beets, cooked and cut into wedges (see steps 1 to 5, page 145). Arrange greens in individual bowls, add quinoa and top with beets. Sprinkle each bowl with 1 tbsp (15 mL) chopped walnuts, if desired.

VARIATIONS

Wilted Kale: Replace the beet greens with an equal amount of trimmed curly kale. In step 2, reduce the pressure cooking time to 2 minutes.

Bacon Greens: Add 2 slices thick-cut bacon, cut into 1-inch (2.5 cm) pieces. In step 5, add bacon to the shimmering oil and cook, stirring, for 3 to 5 minutes or until fat is rendered and bacon is lightly browned. Continue with the remainder of step 5.

Tangy Greens: Add 2 slices thick-cut bacon, cut into 1-inch (2.5 cm) pieces. In step 5, add bacon to the shimmering oil and cook, stirring, for 3 to 5 minutes or until fat is rendered and bacon is lightly browned. Add garlic and hot pepper flakes; cook, stirring, for 1 minute or until fragrant. In a small bowl, combine 1 tbsp (15 mL) granulated sugar, 2 tbsp (30 mL) virgin olive oil and 1 tbsp (15 mL) white wine vinegar; add to the pot along with the greens. Continue with the remainder of step 5.

TIPS

Wash the greens in at least three changes of fresh cold water, making sure all the dirt and grit is removed. Cut off and discard the stem ends.

Four pounds (2 kg) of beets will yield about 1 lb (500 g) of greens. Ask your grocer or farmers' market vendor if they have beet greens that they have cut off the beets for other customers. You can also add Swiss chard to the greens to measure 1 lb (500 g), if necessary.

If your steamer basket doesn't have legs, place a steam rack in the pot first and place the steamer basket on the rack.

Cauliflower, Broccoli and Pickled Red Onion Salad

Pickled red onion adds a unique twist to this cauliflower and broccoli medley. Top it with crumbled bacon for a combination of sweet, salty, tangy and peppery that makes a colorful warm-weather side dish.

MAKES 8 SERVINGS

COOKING PROGRAMS

• Sauté •
• Pressure Cook •

- **Two 1-pint (500 mL) canning jars with lids or glass food storage containers**
- **Steamer basket**

Pickled Onions

2 cups	water	500 mL
1 cup	apple cider vinegar	250 mL
2 tbsp	granulated sugar	30 mL
1 tbsp	salt	15 mL
1	red onion, thinly sliced	1

Salad

1½ tbsp	virgin olive oil	22 mL
5	slices bacon, cut in half	5
2	packages (each 12 oz/340 g) cauliflower and broccoli medley	2
¼ cup	extra virgin olive oil	60 mL
	Salt and freshly ground black pepper	

1. *Pickled Onions:* In a medium bowl, whisk together water, vinegar, sugar and salt until sugar is dissolved. Pack onion slices into canning jars, dividing evenly, and pour half the pickling mixture over each. Cover with lids and let stand at room temperature for 1 hour.

2. *Salad:* Set your Instant Pot to sauté on Normal. When the display says Hot, add virgin olive oil and heat until shimmering. Working in batches, add bacon and cook, turning once, for about 5 minutes or until crispy, transferring bacon to a plate lined with a paper towel as it is cooked. Press Cancel. Let bacon cool to room temperature, then coarsely chop.

3. Drain fat from the pot. Carefully clean the inner pot and return to the cooker.

4. Add 1 cup (250 mL) hot water to the pot. Place the steamer basket in the pot (see tip) and place the cauliflower and broccoli in the basket.

5. Close and lock the lid and turn the steam release handle to Sealing. Set your Instant Pot to pressure cook on High for 0 minutes.

6. When the cooking time is done, press Cancel and turn the steam release handle to Venting. When the float valve drops down, remove the lid. The broccoli and cauliflower should be tender-crisp. (If more cooking time is needed, continue pressure cooking on High for 1 minute.)

7. Transfer vegetables to a bowl of ice water. Drain, transfer to a serving dish and let cool completely.

8. Drizzle cooled vegetables with extra virgin olive oil and season to taste with salt and pepper. Using a fork, lift out as many pickled onions as you like and add on top of the vegetables. Serve sprinkled with bacon.

VARIATION

In place of the pickled onions, use pitted drained black olives.

TIPS

Pickled onions can be stored in their jar in the refrigerator for up to 2 weeks.

Leftover pickled onions are an ideal topping for tacos.

If your steamer basket doesn't have legs, place a steam rack in the pot first and place the steamer basket on the rack.

Ginger and Orange Braised Carrots

Here, carrots are briefly pressure cooked, then simmered down in orange juice and butter for a sweet and tender braised finish with bright citrus notes.

MAKES 6 SERVINGS

COOKING PROGRAMS

• Pressure Cook •
• Sauté •

1½ lbs	carrots, cut diagonally into ½-inch (1 cm) thick slices	750 g
4 tsp	grated gingerroot	20 mL
¾ cup	water	175 mL
½ cup	orange juice, divided	125 mL
3 tbsp	butter, softened, divided	45 mL
	Salt and freshly ground black pepper	
1½ tsp	freshly squeezed lemon juice (optional)	7 mL
	Chopped fresh parsley (optional)	

TIPS

A 1-inch (2.5 cm) square piece of ginger will yield about 4 tsp (20 mL) grated.

For a slightly spicier, herbal tone, substitute ½ tsp (2 mL) ground cardamom for the ginger. Omit the lemon juice.

This recipe can easily be doubled for a large gathering.

1. In the inner pot, combine carrots, ginger, water, ¼ cup (60 mL) orange juice and 1 tbsp (15 mL) butter.

2. Close and lock the lid and turn the steam release handle to Sealing. Set your Instant Pot to pressure cook on High for 2 minutes.

3. When the cooking time is done, press Cancel and turn the steam release handle to Venting. When the float valve drops down, remove the lid. Drain carrots.

4. Set your Instant Pot to sauté on More. When the display says hot, add the remaining butter and heat until melted. Stir in carrots and the remaining orange juice; cook, stirring gently occasionally, for 3 minutes or until liquid has evaporated and carrots are fork-tender.

5. Transfer carrots to a serving bowl and season to taste with salt and pepper. If desired, drizzle with lemon juice and sprinkle with parsley.

Sweet and Easy Corn on the Cob

When the first ears of sweet corn appear at the market, my heart starts pounding with anticipation. This technique for cooking corn in the husks is adapted from a popular microwave version, enabling the ears to just slide out perfectly clean. Serve them plain, buttered or with seasoned butter, and with or without salt.

MAKES 4 SERVINGS

COOKING PROGRAM
• Pressure Cook •

- **Steam rack**

4	ears corn in the husk	4
	Butter or seasoned butter (optional; see variations)	
	Salt	

1. Using a sharp knife, cut off about 3/4 inch (2 cm) of the cob above the stem. Cut tassel end of cob to the tip.

2. Add 1 cup (250 mL) hot water to the inner pot and place the steam rack in the pot. Arrange corn on the rack.

3. Close and lock the lid and turn the steam release handle to Sealing. Set your Instant Pot to pressure cook on High for 2 minutes.

4. When the cooking time is done, press Cancel and turn the steam release handle to Venting. When the float valve drops down, remove the lid. The corn should be tender-crisp. (If more cooking time is needed, continue pressure cooking on High for 1 minute.)

5. Using tongs, remove corn from the pot. Using a water-resistant oven mitt, hot pad or heavy dish towel, grab the pointed end of each ear of corn and, with the larger end pointing down, gently shake and squeeze the ear to slide it out of the husk. Serve immediately, with butter and salt, if desired.

VARIATIONS

Chili Lime Butter: In a small bowl, combine 1/4 cup (60 mL) softened butter, 1 tsp (5 mL) chili powder and 2 tsp (10 mL) freshly squeezed lime juice. For an extra kick, add a pinch of cayenne pepper.

Basil Garlic Parmesan Butter: In a small bowl, combine 1/4 cup (60 mL) softened butter, 1 tbsp (15 mL) finely chopped fresh basil and 1/2 tsp (2 mL) garlic powder. Spread on corn and sprinkle with freshly grated Parmesan cheese.

Chive Dill Butter: In a small bowl, combine 1/4 cup (60 mL) softened butter, 1 tbsp (15 mL) chopped fresh chives, 1 tbsp (15 mL) chopped fresh dill and 1 tsp (5 mL) freshly squeezed lemon juice.

Cajun-Style Butter: In a small bowl, combine 1/4 cup (60 mL) softened butter, 1 tbsp (15 mL) Cajun seasoning and 2 drops of hot pepper sauce (such as Frank's RedHot).

TIPS

You can peel off some of the outside leaves of the husk before cooking if they are tough.

If the ears are long, trim them or cut them in half crosswise to fit in the cooker. Make sure that no leaves or tassels are blocking the release valve.

Green Beans and Pimentos

If you are getting tired of plain old green beans, you needn't look any further for inspiration. Sweet, succulent pimentos add delightful taste and color to simple pressure-cooked beans in the main recipe, and the easy variations give you even more opportunity to mix things up.

MAKES 6 SERVINGS

COOKING PROGRAM

• Pressure Cook •

2 lbs	frozen green beans	1 kg
1	jar (4 oz/114 mL) pimentos, drained	1
1 tsp	garlic powder	5 mL
1 cup	water	250 mL
	Salt	
1 tbsp	extra virgin olive oil	15 mL

TIPS

Substitute fresh green beans, trimmed, for the frozen beans. Decrease the cooking time to 2 minutes.

Mix green and yellow beans for an even more colorful dish.

1. Arrange beans in the inner pot. Add pimentos, garlic powder and water. Season with salt.

2. Close and lock the lid and turn the steam release handle to Sealing. Set your Instant Pot to pressure cook on High for 3 minutes.

3. When the cooking time is done, press Cancel and turn the steam release handle to Venting. When the float valve drops down, remove the lid. The beans should be tender-crisp. (If more cooking time is needed, continue pressure cooking on High for 0 minutes.)

4. Stir beans, drain and transfer to a serving bowl. Drizzle with oil. Serve immediately.

VARIATION

Balsamic Green Beans: Omit the pimentos. Combine 2 tbsp (30 mL) balsamic vinegar, 1 tbsp (15 mL) pure maple syrup and 1 tsp (5 mL) Dijon mustard; set aside. Immediately after step 3, plunge beans in ice water to stop cooking. Drain beans and pat dry. Wipe out pot with a paper towel. Set your Instant Pot to sauté on Normal. When the display says Hot, add 1 tbsp (15 mL) virgin olive oil and heat until shimmering. Add 2 finely chopped shallots and cook, stirring, for 1 minute or until softened. Stir in vinaigrette. Season with salt and pepper. Add green beans and toss to coat with sauce.

VARIATION

Green Beans with Bacon: Omit the pimentos. Before step 1, set your Instant Pot to sauté on Normal. When the display says Hot, add 1 tbsp (15 mL) virgin olive oil and heat until shimmering. Add 4 thick-cut bacon slices, cut into $1/4$-inch (0.5 cm) thick pieces, and 3 thinly sliced shallots; cook, stirring, until bacon fat is rendered and shallots are browned. Press Cancel. Using a slotted spoon, transfer bacon and shallots to a plate. Carefully wipe out pot with a paper towel. Complete steps 1, 2 and 3. In step 4, add the bacon and shallots just before serving.

Summertime Potato Salad

Go to any backyard cookout, and you are sure to see potato salad being served. Variations abound, but the foundation of potatoes, onion and dressing remains the same. This version comes together quickly, without steaming up the kitchen. Make sure to allow for chilling time to meld the flavors.

MAKES 4 SERVINGS

COOKING PROGRAM
• Pressure Cook •

• **Steamer basket**

3	russet potatoes (about 1¾ lbs/ 875 g total), peeled and cut into ¾-inch (2 cm) cubes	3
2	large eggs, in the shell	2
	Ice water	
⅓ cup	finely chopped onion	75 mL
½ cup	mayonnaise (approx.)	125 mL
1 tsp	granulated sugar (optional)	5 mL
2 tsp	prepared yellow mustard	10 mL
	Salt and freshly ground black pepper	

1. Add 1 cup (250 mL) hot water to the inner pot. Place the steamer basket in the pot (see second tip, page 155) and place potatoes and eggs in the basket.

2. Close and lock the lid and turn the steam release handle to Sealing. Set your Instant Pot to pressure cook on High for 4 minutes.

3. When the cooking time is done, press Cancel and turn the steam release handle to Venting. When the float valve drops down, remove the lid. The potatoes should be fork-tender. (If more cooking time is needed, continue pressure cooking on High for 1 minute.) Transfer potatoes to a large bowl and let cool.

4. Transfer eggs to a bowl of ice water to chill, refreshing water as necessary to keep cold. When cool enough to handle, peel and chop eggs.

5. To the potatoes, add onion, mayonnaise, sugar (if using) and mustard, stirring gently to coat. Season to taste with salt and pepper. Gently fold in eggs. Cover and refrigerate for at least 1 hour, until chilled, or for up to 1 day.

6. Just before serving, stir gently, adding more mayonnaise if necessary.

VARIATIONS

Add ½ cup (125 mL) chopped celery in step 5 with the onion.

For a tangier potato salad, stir in 4 tsp (20 mL) pickle juice or relish in step 5 with the mayonnaise.

TIPS

If you prefer, you can substitute plain yogurt for the mayonnaise.

Eggs cooked in the pressure cooker do not need to be aged to make peeling them easier.

You can substitute 6 small red-skinned potatoes for the russets. You do not need to peel them, unless you prefer to do so.

This recipe is easily doubled, so you can take it to your next potluck.

Buttery Garlic Mashed Potatoes

My mother always made the best mashed potatoes. Her secret was loads of butter. This version still has plenty of butter, but with some broth, garlic and cream to round out the flavors.

MAKES 4 SERVINGS

COOKING PROGRAMS

• Pressure Cook •
• Sauté •

• **Steamer basket**

4	russet potatoes (about 1½ lbs/ 750 g total), peeled and cut into 1½-inch (4 cm) pieces	4
5 tbsp	butter, softened, divided	75 mL
3	cloves garlic, minced	3
¼ cup	ready-to-use reduced-sodium chicken broth or Low-Sodium Chicken Stock (variation, page 27)	60 mL
¼ cup	heavy or whipping (35%) cream (approx.)	60 mL
	Salt and freshly ground black pepper	

1. Add 1 cup (250 mL) hot water to the inner pot and place the steamer basket in the pot (see tip). Place potatoes in the basket.

2. Close and lock the lid and turn the steam release handle to Sealing. Set your Instant Pot to pressure cook on High for 8 minutes.

3. When the cooking time is done, press Cancel and turn the steam release handle to Venting. When the float valve drops down, remove the lid. The potatoes should be fork-tender. (If more cooking time is needed, continue pressure cooking on High for 1 minute.) Remove steamer basket and set aside. Discard water.

4. Set your Instant Pot to sauté on Normal. When the display says Hot, add 2 tbsp (30 mL) butter and heat until melted. Add garlic and cook, stirring, for 1 minute or until fragrant. Add potatoes and the remaining butter; start mashing potatoes. When butter is absorbed, add broth, mashing until combined. Press Cancel.

5. Gradually add cream, mashing, until potatoes are your desired consistency. (Use only as much cream as is needed to reach that consistency.) Season to taste with salt and pepper. Transfer to a serving bowl. Serve immediately.

TIPS

You can substitute small yellow-fleshed potatoes, as long as they weigh about 1½ lbs (750 g) total. Reduce the pressure cooking time to 5 minutes. You don't need to peel the potatoes before mashing them.

If your steamer basket doesn't have legs, place a steam rack in the pot first and place the steamer basket on the rack.

Mash potatoes just until they are your desired consistency and everything is combined. Do not overmash.

Braised Red Potatoes

Here, tiny red potatoes are cooked to perfection with garlic and tarragon, braised in a buttery sauce to mimic a roasted finish, then swirled in a garlicky Dijon mixture for a scrumptious taste of heaven.

MAKES 4 SERVINGS

COOKING PROGRAMS

• Pressure Cook •
• Sauté •

1½ lbs	small red-skinned potatoes (about 1½ inches/4 cm in diameter), halved	750 g
3	cloves garlic, peeled	3
2 tbsp	finely chopped fresh tarragon, divided	30 mL
½ tsp	salt	2 mL
¾ cup	ready-to-use reduced-sodium chicken broth or Low-Sodium Chicken Stock (variation, page 27)	175 mL
4 tbsp	butter, divided	60 mL
	Freshly ground black pepper	
2 tsp	Dijon mustard	10 mL

1. In the inner pot, combine potatoes, garlic, 1½ tbsp (22 mL) tarragon, salt, broth and 3 tbsp (45 mL) butter.

2. Close and lock the lid and turn the steam release handle to Sealing. Set your Instant Pot to pressure cook on High for 3 minutes.

3. When the cooking time is done, press Cancel and turn the steam release handle to Venting. When the float valve drops down, remove the lid. The potatoes should be tender but still firm. (If more cooking time is needed, continue pressure cooking on High for 1 minute.)

4. Set your Instant Pot to sauté on Normal. Add the remaining butter and cook, stirring gently occasionally and mashing garlic, for about 10 minutes or until liquid has evaporated and potatoes are sizzling. Press Cancel.

5. Meanwhile, in a small bowl, combine the remaining tarragon, ¼ tsp (1 mL) pepper and mustard.

6. Stir mustard mixture into potatoes until well coated. Season with pepper to taste.

VARIATION

Lemon Chive Potatoes: Omit the tarragon. Add 3 sprigs fresh thyme to the pot in step 1. Before step 4, discard thyme sprigs. Replace the mustard with 1 tbsp (15 mL) lemon juice. In step 6, stir in 2 tbsp (30 mL) minced fresh chives with the lemon juice mixture.

Spanish Potato Tortilla

When a tortilla isn't a tortilla and a main dish is a side dish, I feel like I'm cooking in Wonderland. You'll find this quiche-like potato and onion dish just as delightful and whimsical as Alice's adventures.

MAKES 6 SERVINGS AS A SIDE DISH

COOKING PROGRAMS

• Sauté •
• Pressure Cook •

- **6-cup (1.5 L) casserole dish, well coated with oil**
- **Steam rack**

6	large eggs	6
	Salt	
⅓ cup	virgin olive oil	75 mL
1 lb	yellow-fleshed potatoes, peeled and thinly sliced	500 g
1	onion, thinly sliced	1
2	cloves garlic, minced	2
	Freshly ground black pepper	

1. In the prepared casserole dish, whisk together eggs and ¼ tsp (1 mL) salt until frothy. Set aside.

2. Set your Instant Pot to sauté on Less. When the display says Hot, add oil and heat until shimmering. Add potatoes and cook, stirring often, for 5 minutes. Add onion and cook, stirring often, for 10 minutes or until potatoes and onions are tender. Add garlic and cook, stirring, for 1 minute or until fragrant. Press Cancel. Let stand for 5 minutes.

3. Using a fine-mesh sieve, drain potato mixture, discarding oil. Add to eggs, stirring gently to combine. Season with salt and pepper.

4. Clean and dry the pot and return it to the cooker. Add 1 cup (250 mL) hot water and place the steam rack in the pot. Place a crisscross foil sling (see page 16) on the rack and place the casserole dish in the sling.

5. Close and lock the lid and turn the steam release handle to Sealing. Set your Instant Pot to pressure cook on High for 19 minutes.

6. When the cooking time is done, press Cancel and let stand, covered, for 10 minutes, then turn the steam release handle to Venting. When the float valve drops down, remove the lid. A tester inserted into the tortilla should come out clean (see tip). (If more cooking time is needed, continue pressure cooking on High for 2 minutes, then quickly release the pressure.)

7. Using the foil sling, remove dish from the pot. Serve hot or cooled to room temperature, cut into wedges.

> **TIPS**
>
> This dish serves 4 people as a main course.
>
> When stirring the potatoes and onions in the hot oil, use a long-handled utensil and take care to avoid spattering hot oil.
>
> After the cooking time is done, there may be a slight oily layer on top of the tortilla. Do not be concerned, as this quickly disappears as the tortilla cools and is cut into wedges.

DESSERTS • DESSERTS • DESSERTS
DESSERTS • DESSERTS • DESSERTS
DESSERTS • DESSERTS • DESSERT
ESSERTS • DESSERTS • DESSERTS
DESSERTS • DESSERTS • DESSERT
ESSERTS • DESSERTS • DESSERT
DESSERTS • DESSERTS • DESSERT
ESSERTS • DESSERTS • DESSERTS
DESSERTS • DESSERTS • DESSERT
ESSERTS • DESSERTS • DESSERTS
DESSERTS • DESSERTS • DESSERT
ESSERTS • DESSERTS • DESSERT
DESSERTS • DESSERTS • DESSERT
ESSERTS • DESSERTS • DESSERTS
DESSERTS • DESSERTS • DESSERT
ESSERTS • DESSERTS • DESSERTS

DESSERTS

Fudgy Chocolate Brownies

Cocoa powder makes these brownies extra-chocolaty, and they come out fudgy and moist, for a decadent treat. Serve them warm or at room temperature; either way, they're sure to be a hit.

MAKES 6 TO 8 BROWNIES

COOKING PROGRAM

• Pressure Cook •

- **6-inch (15 cm) springform pan, sprayed with nonstick cooking spray**
- **Steam rack**

²⁄₃ cup	unsweetened cocoa powder	150 mL
½ cup	all-purpose flour	125 mL
¼ tsp	salt	1 mL
1 cup	granulated sugar	250 mL
2	large eggs	2
½ cup	unsalted butter, melted	125 mL

TIPS

You can also use a 6-inch (15 cm) round metal cake pan in this recipe. To make it easier to release the brownies from the pan, line the bottom of the pan with waxed or parchment paper lightly coated with nonstick cooking spray.

Store cooled brownies in an airtight container at room temperature for up to 3 days.

1. In a large bowl, whisk together cocoa, flour and salt.

2. In a medium bowl, whisk together sugar, eggs and butter. Add to the cocoa mixture, whisking well. Pour batter into prepared pan.

3. Add 1 cup (250 mL) hot water to the inner pot and place the steam rack in the pot. Place the pan on the rack.

4. Close and lock the lid and turn the steam release handle to Sealing. Set your Instant Pot to pressure cook on High for 25 minutes.

5. When the cooking time is done, press Cancel and let stand, covered, for 10 minutes, then turn the steam release handle to Venting. When the float valve drops down, remove the lid. A tester inserted in the center should come out with a few moist crumbs clinging to it. (If more cooking time is needed, continue pressure cooking on High for 2 minutes, then quickly release the pressure.)

6. Using the handles of the rack, carefully remove the rack and pan. Let pan cool to room temperature on rack. Remove edges of pan and cut brownie into wedges.

VARIATION

If you have brown sugar that is not dry or lumpy, use ½ cup (125 mL) packed brown sugar in place of half the granulated sugar, for a slightly moister, chewier brownie.

Molten Chocolate Cakes

Chocolate lovers rejoice — these cakes are for you! They're easy to make, but consider yourself warned: it's so hard to wait for them to cool slightly before you dive in with your fork. When the gooey, pudding-like center emerges from the cake dome, you won't be able to keep the smile off your face.

MAKES 4 CAKES

COOKING PROGRAM

• Pressure Cook •

- **Four 6-oz (175 mL) ovenproof custard cups or ramekins, sprayed with nonstick cooking spray**
- **Steam rack**

1 cup	semisweet chocolate chips	250 mL
½ cup	unsalted butter	125 mL
1 cup	confectioners' (icing) sugar	250 mL
3	large eggs	3
1	large egg yolk	1
1 tbsp	vanilla extract	15 mL
6 tbsp	all-purpose flour	90 mL

TIPS

The eggs in this recipe are only lightly cooked. For optimal food safety, use pasteurized in-shell eggs if they are available in your area.

In step 6, if your cakes are sticking to the cups, run a knife around the edge to loosen them before inverting.

You can skip inverting the cakes and simply serve them in the custard cups.

1. In a medium heavy-bottomed saucepan, heat chocolate chips and butter over low heat, stirring until just melted and combined. Remove from heat and stir in confectioners' sugar until smooth.

2. In a small bowl, whisk together eggs, egg yolk and vanilla. Whisk in flour. Pour into chocolate mixture, stirring well. Pour batter into prepared custard cups, dividing evenly.

3. Add 2 cups (500 mL) hot water to the inner pot and place the steam rack in the pot. Arrange the custard cups on the rack, stacking one in the center of the others as needed.

4. Close and lock the lid and turn the steam release handle to Sealing. Set your Instant Pot to pressure cook on High for 11 minutes.

5. When the cooking time is done, press Cancel and turn the steam release handle to Venting. When the float valve drops down, remove the lid. The tops should be firm and dry. (If more cooking time is needed or you prefer a less pudding-like center, continue pressure cooking on High for 1 minute.)

6. Using small silicone oven mitts, carefully remove cups from the pot, run a knife around the edges and invert onto dessert plates. Remove the cups. Let cool slightly and serve warm.

SERVING SUGGESTION

Serve with vanilla ice cream or caramel sauce.

Chocolate Ganache Cake

This dense dark chocolate cake, oozing with sweet custard, is sure to be the pièce de résistance at any celebration. Dust it with confectioners' (icing) sugar or serve each wedge with a dollop of whipped cream.

MAKES 8 SERVINGS

COOKING PROGRAMS

• Sauté •
• Pressure Cook •

- **10-inch (25 cm) or wider mixing bowl**
- **6-inch (15 cm) springform pan, bottom lined with parchment paper, bottom and sides buttered and dusted with unsweetened cocoa powder**
- **Electric mixer**
- **Steam rack**

12 oz	dark chocolate, chopped	375 g
½ cup	unsalted butter, cubed	125 mL
2 tbsp	unsweetened cocoa powder	30 mL
5	large eggs, separated	5
¼ tsp	salt	1 mL
½ cup	granulated sugar	125 mL

1. Add chocolate and butter to the mixing bowl. Set your Instant Pot to sauté on Normal. Add 2 cups (500 mL) hot water to the inner pot and heat until boiling. Place the mixing bowl over the pot, making sure it doesn't touch the water, and heat, stirring, for 2 to 3 minutes or until mixture is half melted. Press Cancel.

2. Remove bowl from heat and stir until melted and smooth (if it is not melting completely, place bowl over the pot of hot water for 1 to 2 minutes and stir until melted). Let cool to room temperature. Reserve water in the pot.

3. Whisk egg yolks into chocolate mixture. Stir in cocoa powder.

4. In a medium bowl, using the electric mixer, beat eggs whites and salt until frothy. Gradually add sugar, beating until medium-firm peaks form.

5. Fold one-third of the egg whites into the chocolate mixture until blended, then gently fold in the remaining egg whites just until incorporated. Pour mixture into prepared pan and smooth top.

6. Place the steam rack in the pot and place the pan on the rack.

7. Close and lock the lid and turn the steam release handle to Sealing. Set your Instant Pot to pressure cook on High for 12 minutes.

8. When the cooking time is done, press Cancel and turn the steam release handle to Venting. When the float valve drops down, remove the lid. The top and sides of the cake should be set and it should be slightly jiggly in the center. (If more cooking time is needed, continue pressure cooking on High for 2 minutes.)

9. Using the handles of the rack, carefully remove rack and pan. Let pan cool on rack for 1 hour. Refrigerate for at least 4 hours or overnight before removing cake from the pan. Cut into 8 wedges.

> **TIP**
>
> Do not be concerned if this cake falls in the center — that is typical.

New York–Style Cheesecake

You must have seen photos online of Instant Pot cheesecakes. That may even be the reason you bought an IP. Well, there's a good reason for all that excitement: they consistently turn out firm and just plain scrumptious.

MAKES 8 SERVINGS

COOKING PROGRAM

• Pressure Cook •

- **6-inch (15 cm) springform pan, buttered**
- **Food processor**
- **Steam rack**

1¼ cups	graham cracker crumbs	300 mL
¼ cup	unsalted butter, melted	60 mL
1 lb	brick-style cream cheese, softened	500 g
⅔ cup	granulated sugar	150 mL
2	large eggs, at room temperature	2
1 tsp	vanilla extract	5 mL

1. In a small bowl, combine graham cracker crumbs and butter until evenly moist. Press into the bottom and halfway up the sides of prepared pan.

2. In food processor, process cream cheese and sugar until smooth, scraping down the sides of the bowl as needed. With the motor running, add eggs through the feed tube and process until smooth. Add vanilla and process for 2 minutes or until smooth and creamy. Pour batter over crust.

3. Add 1½ cups (375 mL) hot water to the inner pot and place the steam rack in the pot. Place the pan on the rack.

4. Close and lock the lid and turn the steam release handle to Sealing. Set your Instant Pot to pressure cook on High for 25 minutes.

5. When the cooking time is done, press Cancel. Let stand, covered, until the float valve drops down, then remove the lid. A tester inserted in the center should come out clean. (If more cooking time is needed, continue pressure cooking on High for 5 minutes, then quickly release the pressure.)

6. Using the handles of the rack, carefully remove the rack and pan. Let pan cool on rack for 1 hour, then remove edges of pan. Cover and refrigerate cake for at least 6 hours or up to 2 days before cutting.

SERVING SUGGESTION

Serve topped with your favorite berries.

VARIATION

Instead of the graham cracker crumbs, use crushed vanilla or chocolate wafers, shortbread cookies or gingersnaps.

TIP

The cheesecake can be covered and refrigerated for up to 1 week. When covering, make sure there is a gap between the cake and the cover, to prevent any sticking.

Blueberry Cake with Lemon Glaze

Blueberries and lemon remind me of the beloved characters Raggedy Ann and Andy — different they may be, but when they get together, they make a spirited duo.

MAKES 8 SERVINGS		

COOKING PROGRAM

• Pressure Cook •

- **7-inch (18 cm) nonstick fluted tube pan (such as a Bundt or kugelhopf), sprayed with nonstick cooking spray**
- **Steam rack**

2 cups	blueberry muffin mix with real blueberries (about 12½ oz/375 g)	500 mL
2	large eggs	2
⅓ cup	water	75 mL
⅓ cup	vegetable oil	75 mL
1 cup	confectioners' (icing) sugar (approx.)	250 mL
3 tbsp	freshly squeezed lemon juice (approx.)	45 mL

1. In a medium bowl, combine muffin mix, eggs, water and oil, stirring just until combined. Pour into prepared pan. Spray a piece of foil with nonstick cooking spray and cover pan with foil, spray side down, forming a slightly rounded top and sealing edges tightly.

2. Add 2 cups (500 mL) hot water to the inner pot and place the steam rack in the pot. Place a crisscross foil sling (see page 16) on the rack and place the pan in the sling.

3. Close and lock the lid and turn the steam release handle to Sealing. Set your Instant Pot to pressure cook on High for 25 minutes.

4. When the cooking time is done, press Cancel and let stand, covered, for 10 minutes, then turn the steam release handle to Venting. When the float valve drops down, remove the lid. Carefully peel back foil. A tester inserted in the center should come out clean. (If more cooking time is needed, continue pressure cooking on High for 5 minutes, then quickly release the pressure.)

5. Using the foil sling, remove pan from the pot. Remove rack from the pot, return pan to rack and let cool for 10 minutes, then invert cake onto the rack to cool completely.

6. Meanwhile, in a glass measuring cup, combine ¾ cup (175 mL) confectioners' sugar and 2 tbsp (30 mL) lemon juice until smooth. Gradually add more sugar and lemon juice until glaze is thick but easy to pour.

7. Drizzle glaze over cake. Let stand until set. Cut into slices and serve.

VARIATION

Grate some lemon zest before squeezing the lemon. Sprinkle the zest on top of the cake before slicing.

TIPS

If your muffin mix contains real blueberries in a separate can or bag, follow the package instructions for draining or rehydrating them and add them with the mix in step 1. Use about 3 tbsp (45 mL) drained canned or rehydrated blueberries. Do not use a mix made with imitation blueberries.

In step 6, using a container with a pour spout, such as a 2-cup (500 mL) glass measuring cup, will make drizzling the glaze easier.

You may want to place a foil sheet under the wire rack before drizzling the cake with glaze in step 7, to collect any glaze that drizzles off of the cake.

The cake can be stored in an airtight container at room temperature for up to 4 days.

Blueberry Blintz Soufflé

Imagine a thin crêpe enclosing an incredible berry filling, and you're picturing a blintz. Now imagine that you take it one step further and surround several blintzes with a sweet, creamy egg batter. What would you have? Why, a simple, light dessert with delight in every bite.

MAKES 6 SERVINGS

COOKING PROGRAM

• Pressure Cook •

- **6-cup (1.5 L) round soufflé dish**
- **Electric mixer**
- **Steam rack**

2 tbsp	butter, melted	30 mL
6	frozen blueberry blintzes (about 13 oz/368 g total)	6
3 tbsp	granulated sugar	45 mL
3	large eggs	3
1 cup	sour cream	250 mL
1 tbsp	orange juice	15 mL

TIPS

Blintzes can be found in the freezer section, near kosher foods, in well-stocked grocery stores or in either the refrigerated or frozen sections of specialty kosher stores and big-box grocery stores. If using refrigerated blintzes, decrease the cooking time in step 4 to 26 minutes.

Leftovers can be stored in an airtight container in the refrigerator for up to 3 days.

1. Add butter to soufflé dish. Roll blintzes in butter and arrange them in a single layer.

2. In a medium bowl, using the electric mixer, beat sugar, eggs, sour cream and orange juice until sugar is dissolved and mixture is smooth. Pour over blintzes.

3. Add 1½ cups (375 mL) hot water to the inner pot and place the steam rack in the pot. Place a crisscross foil sling (see page 16) on the rack and place the soufflé dish in the sling.

4. Close and lock the lid and turn the steam release handle to Sealing. Set your Instant Pot to pressure cook on High for 30 minutes.

5. When the cooking time is done, press Cancel and let stand, covered, until the float valve drops down, then remove the lid. A tester inserted in the middle should come out slightly wet but clean. (If more cooking time is needed, continue pressure cooking on High for 5 minutes, then quickly release the pressure.)

6. Using the foil sling, remove dish from the pot. Remove rack from the pot, return dish to rack and let cool for 15 minutes, then cut soufflé into 6 wedges.

VARIATION

Substitute cherry blintzes for the blueberry blintzes.

Homestyle Bread Pudding

This is a fabulous way to turn leftovers into a delightful dessert — or, better yet, to turn dessert into a breakfast treat! However you serve it, you are sure to enjoy this rich, hassle-free bread pudding. You can even toss in some spices, nuts or chocolate chunks for a different twist. Serve topped with dollops of whipped cream, if desired.

MAKES 6 SERVINGS

COOKING PROGRAM

• Pressure Cook •

- **4-cup (1 L) round soufflé dish, bottom and sides buttered**
- **Steam rack**

3 tbsp	unsalted butter, softened	45 mL
1 lb	sweet egg bread (such as challah or brioche), crusts trimmed off	500 g
3	large eggs	3
1/3 cup	granulated sugar	75 mL
1½ cups	half-and-half (10%) cream	375 mL
2 tsp	vanilla extract	10 mL

1. Butter both sides of bread slices and cut into 2-inch (5 cm) square pieces. You should have about 6 cups (1.5 L).

2. In a large bowl, whisk eggs. Whisk in sugar, cream and vanilla. Fold in bread pieces, gently pressing down on bread to cover with liquid. Let stand for 30 minutes or until bread has absorbed liquid.

3. Pour bread mixture into prepared soufflé dish. Add 1 cup (250 mL) hot water to the inner pot and place the steam rack in the pot. Place the soufflé dish on the rack and cover with foil.

4. Close and lock the lid and turn the steam release handle to Sealing. Set your Instant Pot to pressure cook on High for 30 minutes.

5. When the cooking time is done, press Cancel and turn the steam release handle to Venting. When the float valve drops down, remove the lid. A tester inserted in the center should come out clean. (If more cooking time is needed, continue pressure cooking on High for 5 minutes.)

6. Using the handles of the rack, carefully remove rack and dish. Remove foil and let stand at room temperature for at least 10 minutes or up to 2 hours.

VARIATIONS

Spiced Bread Pudding: Add 1 tsp (5 mL) ground cinnamon, nutmeg or cardamom with the sugar in step 2.

Chocolate Chip Bread Pudding: In step 3, add half of the bread and egg mixture to the dish. Sprinkle with ½ cup (125 mL) chocolate chips, then add the remaining bread and egg mixture. Continue as directed.

Nutty Bread Pudding: In step 3, add half of the bread and egg mixture to the dish. Sprinkle with ½ cup (125 mL) chopped nuts, then add the remaining bread and egg mixture. Continue as directed.

TIPS

If you prefer to keep the crust on the bread, use 12 oz (375 g) bread.

Leftover bread pudding can be stored in an airtight container in the refrigerator for up to 3 days.

Maple Rice Pudding

Rice pudding is an old-time favorite comfort food. Add some maple syrup and a hint of cinnamon, and you will swoon over the results.

MAKES 6 SERVINGS		
COOKING PROGRAMS		
• Sauté •		
• Pressure Cook •		

2 tbsp	unsalted butter, divided	30 mL
1 cup	Arborio or other short-grain white rice	250 mL
⅛ tsp	salt	0.5 mL
2 cups	water	500 mL
1½ cups	milk, divided	375 mL
½ tsp	vanilla extract	2 mL
⅓ cup	pure maple syrup	75 mL
	Ground cinnamon	

> ### TIP
> Leftover rice pudding can be stored in an airtight container in the refrigerator for up to 4 days.

1. Set your Instant Pot to sauté on Normal. When the display says Hot, add 1 tbsp (15 mL) butter and heat until melted. Add rice and cook, stirring, for 1 to 2 minutes or until rice is coated with butter and starting to crackle. Press Cancel. Stir in salt, water, 1 cup (250 mL) milk and vanilla.

2. Close and lock the lid and turn the steam release handle to Sealing. Set your Instant Pot to pressure cook on High for 7 minutes.

3. When the cooking time is done, press Cancel and let stand, covered, for 5 minutes, then turn the steam release handle to Venting. When the float valve drops down, remove the lid. The rice should be tender. (If more cooking time is needed, continue pressure cooking on High for 1 minute, then quickly release the pressure.)

4. Stir in the remaining milk, maple syrup and the remaining butter. Press Sauté until Less is highlighted and cook, stirring often, for 3 minutes or until pudding is slightly thickened. (Note: it will continue to thicken after it is removed from the heat.) Serve sprinkled with cinnamon.

VARIATIONS

Maple Rice Pudding with Dried Fruit: Add ⅓ cup (75 mL) raisins or dried cranberries with the maple syrup in step 4.

Substitute ½ cup (125 mL) granulated sugar for the maple syrup.

Garnish with ground cardamom instead of cinnamon.

Chocolate Pots de Crème

A creamy, dense custard steeped in rich dark chocolate can momentarily make you feel like you haven't a care in the world. Some may call this chocolate pudding, but I would call it chocolate euphoria.

MAKES 6 SERVINGS

COOKING PROGRAM

• Pressure Cook •

- **Six 4-oz (125 mL) ramekins**
- **Steam rack**

6 oz	bittersweet (dark) chocolate block	175 g
2 cups	half-and-half (10%) cream	500 mL
Pinch	salt	Pinch
3 tbsp	granulated sugar	45 mL
6	large egg yolks	6
1 tsp	vanilla extract	5 mL
	Whipped cream (optional)	

1. Using a vegetable peeler or sharp knife, cut one-quarter of the chocolate block into thin shavings. Set aside. Finely chop the remaining chocolate and place in a large bowl.

2. In a small saucepan, combine cream and salt; bring just to a boil over medium-high heat, stirring often. Pour over chopped chocolate and let stand for 3 minutes, then whisk until chocolate is melted and well combined.

3. In a small bowl, whisk together sugar and egg yolks. Whisk into chocolate mixture. Stir in vanilla.

4. Strain through a fine-mesh sieve into a measuring cup or container with a spout. Pour into ramekins, dividing evenly. Cover ramekins with foil, pinching tightly around the sides.

5. Add 2 cups (500 mL) hot water to the inner pot and place the steam rack in the pot. Arrange the ramekins on the rack, stacking them in alternating layers (like stacking bricks).

6. Close and lock the lid and turn the steam release handle to Sealing. Set your Instant Pot to pressure cook on High for 5 minutes.

7. When the cooking time is done, press Cancel and let stand, covered, until the float valve drops down, then remove the lid. Carefully remove a ramekin and remove the foil. The custard should be set but still a little jiggly. (If more cooking time is needed, recover and continue pressure cooking on High for 1 minute, then quickly release the pressure.)

8. Carefully remove ramekins from the pot and remove foil. Let cool for 5 minutes and serve warm, or let cool completely and serve cool or chilled. If desired, add a dollop of whipped cream to each. Serve garnished with chocolate shavings.

> **TIP**
>
> The cooled pots de crème can be covered and refrigerated for up to 2 days. They taste even better chilled than warm.

Classic Caramel Flan

What could possibly make a simple flan — creamy egg pudding topped with decadent caramel — even better? That's easy: a simple cooking method in the Instant Pot!

MAKES 6 SERVINGS

COOKING PROGRAM

• Pressure Cook •

- **6-cup (1.5 L) round soufflé dish (7-inch/18 cm diameter)**
- **Steam rack**

³⁄₄ cup	granulated sugar, divided	175 mL
	Water	
1 cup	milk	250 mL
1 cup	heavy or whipping (35%) cream	250 mL
Pinch	salt	Pinch
2 tsp	vanilla extract	10 mL
3	large eggs	3

1. In a small saucepan, combine ½ cup (125 mL) sugar and 2 tbsp (30 mL) water. Bring to a boil over medium-high heat, stirring to dissolve sugar. Boil, moving pan frequently but without stirring, for about 5 minutes or until mixture becomes a light brown caramel color.

2. Pour caramel into soufflé dish, tilting the dish so the caramel coats the bottom. Set aside to cool.

3. In a medium saucepan, combine milk and cream; cook over medium heat for about 3 minutes or until just starting to form bubbles around the edges. Add the remaining sugar, salt and vanilla; cook, stirring, for about 1 minute or until sugar is dissolved. Remove from heat.

4. In a medium bowl, whisk eggs until blended. Gradually pour hot milk mixture into eggs in a thin, steady stream, whisking continuously. Strain through a fine-mesh sieve into soufflé dish.

5. Add 1½ cups (375 mL) hot water to the inner pot and place the steam rack in the pot. Place a crisscross foil sling (see page 16) on the rack and place the soufflé dish in the sling.

6. Close and lock the lid and turn the steam release handle to Sealing. Set your Instant Pot to pressure cook on High for 12 minutes.

7. When the cooking time is done, press Cancel and let stand, covered, until the float valve drops down. Turn the steam release handle to Venting and remove the lid. The custard should be set around the edges and just slightly jiggly in the center. It may be slightly bubbly around the top and edges. (If more cooking time is needed, continue pressure cooking on High for 2 minutes, then quickly release the pressure.)

8. Using the foil sling, remove dish from the pot. Remove rack from the pot, return dish to the rack and let cool completely. Cover and refrigerate for at least 6 hours, until set, or up to 3 days.

9. Run a knife around edges of flan. Invert a deep serving platter over the dish and invert both platter and dish, transferring the flan to the platter. Serve chilled.

Decadent Crème Brûlée

This recipe gives you results that are just as good as the efforts of any fancy restaurant.

MAKES 6 SERVINGS

COOKING PROGRAM

• Pressure Cook •

- **Six 4-oz (125 mL) ramekins**
- **Steam rack**
- **Blender or small food processor**
- **Kitchen torch (see tip)**

⅓ cup	granulated sugar	75 mL
6	large egg yolks (see third tip, page 138)	6
1 cup	heavy or whipping (35%) cream	250 mL
1 cup	half-and-half (10%) cream	250 mL
2 tsp	vanilla extract	10 mL
3 tbsp	granulated sugar	45 mL

1. In a large bowl, whisk together ⅓ cup (75 mL) sugar and egg yolks. Whisk in heavy cream, half-and-half cream and vanilla until just combined.

2. Strain through a fine-mesh sieve into a measuring cup or container with a spout. Pour into ramekins, dividing evenly. Cover ramekins with foil, pinching tightly around the sides.

3. Add 1½ cups (375 mL) hot water to the inner pot and place the steam rack in the pot. Arrange the ramekins on the rack, stacking them in alternating layers (like stacking bricks).

4. Close and lock the lid and turn the steam release handle to Sealing. Set your Instant Pot to pressure cook on High for 6 minutes.

5. When the cooking time is done, press Cancel and let stand, covered, for 10 minutes, then turn the steam release handle to Venting. When the float valve drops down, remove the lid. A knife inserted in the center should come out clean. (If more cooking time is needed, continue pressure cooking on High for 2 minutes, then quickly release the pressure.)

6. Transfer ramekins to a baking sheet and remove foil. Let cool for 30 minutes, then cover with plastic wrap and refrigerate for at least 2 hours, until chilled, or for up to 3 days.

7. In blender, pulse 3 tbsp (45 mL) sugar until very fine.

8. Sprinkle sugar evenly over each custard. Using the torch, brown tops until sugar is evenly melted and caramelized. Let cool for 5 to 10 minutes or until sugar has hardened. Serve immediately.

VARIATION

Berry-Topped Crème Brûlée: Omit the 3 tbsp (45 mL) sugar and skip steps 7 and 8. Top the custards with your favorite berries.

TIP

If you don't have a kitchen torch, preheat the broiler, with the rack 4 inches (10 cm) from the heat source. After sprinkling the custards with sugar, broil for about 5 minutes, watching carefully and rotating as needed.

Key Lime Pie

Originating in the Florida Keys, this famous pie has seen many iterations, but its true heart — a combination of Key limes and a sweet cream custard — remains the same. Serve it dolloped with whipped cream, if desired.

MAKES 6 SERVINGS

COOKING PROGRAM
• Pressure Cook •

- **6-inch (15 cm) springform pan, buttered**
- **Steam rack**

12	Key limes (approx.)	12
1¼ cups	graham cracker crumbs	300 mL
¼ cup	unsalted butter, melted	60 mL
3	large egg yolks	3
1	can (14 oz or 300 mL) sweetened condensed milk	1

1. Grate 2 tsp (10 mL) zest from limes and squeeze ½ cup (125 mL) juice.

2. In a small bowl, combine graham cracker crumbs and butter until evenly moist. Press into the bottom and about 1¼ inches (3 cm) up the sides of prepared pan.

3. In a large bowl, whisk egg yolks until paler in color. Add milk, lime zest and lime juice, whisking until well blended and frothy. Pour batter over crust and cover tightly with foil.

4. Add 1 cup (250 mL) hot water to the inner pot and place the steam rack in the pot. Place the pan on the rack.

5. Close and lock the lid and turn the steam release handle to Sealing. Set your Instant Pot to pressure cook on High for 22 minutes.

6. When the cooking time is done, press Cancel and let stand, covered, for 10 minutes, then turn the steam release handle to Venting. When the float valve drops down, remove the lid. A knife inserted in the center should come out clean. (If more cooking time is needed, continue pressure cooking on High for 4 minutes, then quickly release the pressure.)

7. Using the handles of the rack, carefully remove rack and pan. Remove foil and let pan cool on rack. Cover and refrigerate pie for at least 4 hours or up to 3 days.

VARIATION

Meringue Topping: While the pie is cooking, in a medium bowl, using a handheld electric mixer, beat 3 egg whites until soft peaks form. In a small bowl, combine 1/3 cup (75 mL) granulated sugar, 1/2 tsp (2 mL) cornstarch and a pinch of salt. Gradually add the sugar mixture to the egg whites, beating until sugar is dissolved. Spoon meringue over the hot pie, spreading it to the edges, immediately after removing the pie from the pot in step 7. Brown under a preheated broiler or with a kitchen torch, if desired. Cool and chill, uncovered, as directed.

TIP

If you are unable to find fresh Key limes, you can use 1/2 cup (125 mL) bottled juice, often called Key West lime juice (not Key lime juice). It can be found with the bottles of lemon and lime juice in your grocery store. Grate 2 tsp (10 mL) zest from regular (Persian) limes.

Mini Pumpkin Pies

Your guests will love being served their own mini pumpkin pies. These creamy, light and delightful little gems don't have a crust, so they are less fussy to make, but still scrumptious. Serve each with a dollop of whipped cream, if desired.

MAKES 8 SERVINGS

COOKING PROGRAM

• Pressure Cook •

- **Eight 4-oz (125 mL) ramekins**
- **Steam rack**
- **Tall steam rack (see tip)**

2	large eggs	2
1 tbsp	cornstarch	15 mL
2½ tsp	pumpkin pie spice	12 mL
Pinch	salt	Pinch
½ tsp	vanilla extract (optional)	2 mL
1	can (14 oz or 300 mL) sweetened condensed milk	1
1	can (15 oz/426 mL) pumpkin purée (not pie filling)	1

TIPS

If you don't have a tall steam rack, you can stack the ramekins on the rack in alternating layers (like stacking bricks). The pies on the bottom layer may not be as smooth on top, but they will be just as delicious.

Remove the lid carefully in step 4 to avoid dripping any moisture from the lid onto the pies.

The pies can be cooled, covered tightly and refrigerated for up to 3 days.

1. In a large bowl, whisk eggs. Whisk in cornstarch, pie spice, salt, vanilla (if using) and milk until well combined. Stir in pumpkin until thoroughly combined. Pour into ramekins, dividing evenly.

2. Add 1½ cups (375 mL) hot water to the inner pot and place the steam rack in the pot. Arrange 4 ramekins on the rack. Place the tall steam rack over the ramekins and place the remaining ramekins on top.

3. Close and lock the lid and turn the steam release handle to Sealing. Set your Instant Pot to pressure cook on High for 9 minutes.

4. When the cooking time is done, press Cancel and let stand, covered, for 10 minutes, then turn the steam release handle to Venting. When the float valve drops down, remove the lid. A tester inserted in the center of a ramekin should come out clean. (If more cooking time is needed, continue pressure cooking on High for 2 minutes, then quickly release the pressure.)

5. Carefully remove ramekins from the pot and let cool to room temperature.

SERVING SUGGESTION

Serve with graham crackers or shortbread cookies.

Lip-Smacking Peach Cobbler

When lip-smacking, chin-dripping peaches are in season, there is nothing like a wonderfully tasty cobbler. Serve it warm, with a scoop of vanilla ice cream.

MAKES 6 SERVINGS

COOKING PROGRAM

• Pressure Cook •

- **6-cup (1.5 L) round soufflé dish, bottom and sides buttered**
- **Steam rack**

5	peaches, peeled (see tip) and sliced (about 2½ cups/625 mL)	5
1½ cups	all-purpose baking mix (such as Bisquick)	375 mL
½ cup	packed brown sugar, divided	125 mL
¼ tsp	ground nutmeg	1 mL
1 cup	milk	250 mL

1. Arrange peaches, with any accumulated juices, in prepared soufflé dish.

2. In a medium bowl, whisk together baking mix, ⅓ cup (75 mL) brown sugar and nutmeg. Whisk in milk just until moistened and a few lumps remain. Pour evenly over peaches.

3. Add 1½ cups (375 mL) hot water to the inner pot and place the steam rack in the pot. Place a crisscross foil sling (see page 16) on the rack and place the soufflé dish in the sling.

4. Close and lock the lid and turn the steam release handle to Sealing. Set your Instant Pot to pressure cook on High for 20 minutes.

5. When the cooking time is done, press Cancel and let stand, covered, for 10 minutes, then turn the steam release handle to Venting. When the float valve drops down, remove the lid and foil. A tester inserted in the center of the cobbler should come out clean. (If more cooking time is needed, continue pressure cooking on High for 2 minutes, then quickly release the pressure.)

6. Meanwhile, preheat broiler with rack about 7 inches (18 cm) from the heat.

7. Using the foil sling, remove dish from the pot. Sprinkle with the remaining brown sugar. Broil for about 5 minutes or until topping is browned. Let cool on rack and serve warm or at room temperature.

TIPS

To quickly peel peaches, fill the inner pot halfway with water. Set your Instant Pot to sauté on Normal. When the water is boiling, use tongs to dunk each peach in the water for 10 to 20 seconds or until the skin starts to split. Quickly plunge peach in a bowl of ice water. Use your fingers to peel the skin off the peaches. Reserve 1½ cups (375 mL) water in the pot for step 3 and discard the remainder.

You can use 2½ cups (625 mL) frozen sliced peaches, thawed, in place of fresh. Combine the peaches with 3 tbsp (45 mL) orange juice or water before adding them to the soufflé dish.

INSTANT POT'S COOKING TIME TABLES

||||||||||||||||||||||||||||||||||||||||||||||||||||||||||||||||||||||||||||||||||||||||||||||||||||||||||||||||

AS WITH conventional cooking, cooking with the Instant Pot is full of personal choices, creativity, a lot of science and experimentation. No two individuals have exactly the same tastes or preferences for the tenderness and texture of food. The following cooking time tables are for your reference only and provide a general guideline on the length of pressure-cooking time for various foods. We encourage you to experiment to find the settings for the best results for your own preferences.

There are other factors that may affect the cooking time. Different cuts of meat and different types of rice, for example, may require a different cooking time to yield the same tenderness or texture.

The times indicated in the tables are based on a cooking pressure in the range of 10.15 to 11.6 psi.

MEAT (BEEF, LAMB, PORK, POULTRY)

There are a few things to be aware of when cooking meat:

- Raw meat is perishable and should not be left at room temperature for more than 2 hours (or 1 hour if room temperature is above 32°C (90°F). When using the Delay Start program, do not set time for more than 1 to 2 hours. We recommend to precook meat and select the Keep Warm or Warm program to maintain the food at the correct serving temperature.

- Do not try to thicken the sauce before cooking. Cornstarch, flour or arrowroot may deposit on the bottom of the inner pot and block heat dissipation. As a result, the pressure cooker may overheat.

- You may want to brown or sear the meat by selecting the Sauté program to seal the juices before pressure cooking.

MEAT	COOKING TIME
Beef (pot roast, steak, rump, round, chuck, blade or brisket), small chunks	15–20 minutes per 1 lb (450 g)
Beef (pot roast, steak, rump, round, chuck, blade or brisket), large chunks	20–25 minutes per 1 lb (450 g)
Beef, dressed	20–25 minutes per 1 lb (450 g)
Beef, meatballs	5 minutes per 1 lb (450 g)
Beef, oxtail	40–50 minutes
Beef, ribs	20–25 minutes
Beef, shanks	25–30 minutes
Beef, stew meat	20 minutes per 1 lb (450 g)
Chicken, bone stock	40–50 minutes
Chicken, breasts (boneless)	6–8 minutes
Chicken, cut, with bones	10–15 minutes
Chicken, whole (4–5 lbs/2–2.5 kg)	8 minutes per 1 lb (450 g)
Duck, portions with bones	12–15 minutes
Duck, whole	10 – 15 minutes per 1 lb (450 g)
Ham, picnic shoulder	8 minutes per 1 lb (450 g)
Ham, slices	9–12 minutes
Lamb, cubes	10–15 minutes
Lamb, leg	15 minutes per 1 lb (450 g)
Lamb, stew meat	12–15 minutes
Pheasant	8 minutes per 1 lb (450 g)
Pork, butt roast	15 minutes per 1 lb (450 g)
Pork, loin roast	20 minutes per 1 lb (450 g)
Pork, ribs	15–20 minutes
Quail, whole	8 minutes per 1 lb (450 g)
Turkey, breast (boneless)	7–9 minutes
Turkey, breast (whole)	20–25 minutes
Turkey, drumsticks (leg)	15–20 minutes
Veal, chops	5–8 minutes
Veal, roast	12 minutes per 1 lb (450 g)

SEAFOOD AND FISH

The cooking time for seafood is typically short. The best result is achieved with the original juice being retained in the food. Steaming is the ideal cooking method; however, stewing the food will also produce great results.

When steaming seafood, you will need at least 1 cup (250 mL) of water and an ovenproof or steel bowl on a steam rack. When seafood or fish is overcooked, the texture becomes tough; to avoid this, you should control the cooking time. Normally, you'll need to use the steam release handle to release the pressure and stop cooking as soon as the programmed cooking period is over. An alternative is to take the natural cooking time (7 to 10 minutes) into consideration.

SEAFOOD AND FISH	FRESH COOKING TIME	FROZEN COOKING TIME
Crab, whole	2–3 minutes	4–5 minutes
Fish, fillet	2–3 minutes	3–4 minutes
Fish, steak	3–4 minutes	4–6 minutes
Fish, whole	4–5 minutes	5–7 minutes
Lobster	2–3 minutes	3–4 minutes
Mussels	1–2 minutes	2–3 minutes
Seafood soup or stock	7–8 minutes	8–9 minutes
Shrimp or prawns	1–3 minutes	2–4 minutes

DRIED LEGUMES

There are a few things to be aware of when cooking dried beans, peas and lentils:

- Dried beans double in volume and weight after soaking or cooking. To avoid overflow, fill the inner pot no more than halfway, to allow room for expansion.
- When cooking dried beans, use sufficient liquid to cover the beans.
- Although soaking dried beans is not necessary, it can speed up cooking significantly. Immerse the beans in four times their volume of water for 4 to 6 hours.

If beans and legumes are undercooked, their texture is unpleasant. Consider the cooking times below to be minimum times.

DRIED BEAN, PEA OR LENTIL	DRIED COOKING TIME	SOAKED COOKING TIME
Adzuki beans	16–20 minutes	4–6 minutes
Anasazi beans	20–25 minutes	5–7 minutes
Black beans	20–25 minutes	6–8 minutes
Black-eyed peas	14–18 minutes	4–5 minutes
Chickpeas (garbanzo beans)	35–40 minutes	10–15 minutes
Cannellini (white kidney) beans	30–35 minutes	6–9 minutes
Great Northern beans	25–30 minutes	7–8 minutes
Lentils, brown	8–10 minutes	n/a
Lentils, green	8–10 minutes	n/a
Lentils, red, split	1–2 minutes	n/a
Lentils, yellow, split	1–2 minutes	n/a
Lima beans	12–14 minutes	6–10 minutes
Navy (white pea) beans	20–25 minutes	7–8 minutes
Pinto beans	25–30 minutes	6–9 minutes
Peas	16–20 minutes	10–12 minutes
Red kidney beans	15–20 minutes	7–8 minutes
Scarlet runner beans	20–25 minutes	6–8 minutes
Soybeans	35–45 minutes	18–20 minutes

RICE AND OTHER GRAINS

For rice and other grains, use the grain-to-water ratios in the following chart. The rice measuring cup (180 mL) provided with your Instant Pot can be used to measure the ratios. One cup of grain yields approximately one adult serving.

GRAIN	WATER QUANTITY RATIO (GRAIN TO WATER)	COOKING TIME
Barley, pearl	1:2.5	20–22 minutes
Barley, pot	1:3 to 1:4	25–30 minutes
Congee, thick	1:4 to 1:5	15–20 minutes
Congee, thin	1:6 to 1:7	15–20 minutes
Couscous	1:2	2–3 minutes
Corn, dried/halved	1:3	5–6 minutes
Kamut, whole	1:2	10–12 minutes
Millet	1:1.75	10–12 minutes
Oats, quick-cooking	1:2	2–3 minutes
Oats, steel-cut	1:3	3–5 minutes
Porridge, thin	1:6 to 1:7	5–7 minutes
Quinoa, quick-cooking	1:1.25	1 minute
Rice, basmati	1:1	4 minutes
Rice, brown	1:1	20–22 minutes
Rice, jasmine	1:1	4 minutes
Rice, white	1:1	4 minutes
Rice, wild	1:2	20–25 minutes
Sorghum	1:3	20–25 minutes
Spelt berries (unsoaked)	1:1.5	25–30 minutes
Wheat berries (unsoaked)	1:3	25–30 minutes

VEGETABLES

When steaming vegetables, you will require 1 cup (250 mL) of water and an ovenproof or steel bowl on a steam rack. When cooking vegetables, fresh or frozen, we recommend using the Steam program to preserve the maximum amount of vitamins and minerals. Steaming also retains the natural look of the vegetables.

VEGETABLES	FRESH COOKING TIME	FROZEN COOKING TIME
Artichoke, hearts	4–5 minutes	5–6 minutes
Artichoke, whole, trimmed	9–11 minutes	11–13 minutes
Asparagus, whole or cut	1–2 minutes	2–3 minutes
Beans, green, yellow or wax, ends trimmed and strings removed	1–2 minutes	2–3 minutes
Beet, large, whole	20–25 minutes	25–30 minutes
Beet, small, whole	11–13 minutes	13–15 minutes
Bell pepper, slices or chunks	1–3 minutes	2–4 minutes
Broccoli, florets	1–2 minutes	2–3 minutes
Broccoli, stalks	3–4 minutes	4–5 minutes
Brussels sprouts, whole	2–3 minutes	3–4 minutes
Cabbage, red, purple or green, shredded	2–3 minutes	3–4 minutes
Cabbage, red, purple or green, wedges	3–4 minutes	4–5 minutes
Carrots, sliced or shredded	2–3 minutes	3–4 minutes
Carrots, whole or chunks	6–8 minutes	7–9 minutes
Cauliflower, florets	2–3 minutes	3–4 minutes
Celery, chunks	2–3 minutes	3–4 minutes
Collard greens	4–5 minutes	5–6 minutes
Corn, kernels	1–2 minutes	2–3 minutes
Corn, on the cob	3–5 minutes	4–6 minutes
Eggplant, slices or chunks	3–4 minutes	3–4 minutes
Endive	1–2 minutes	2–3 minutes
Escarole, chopped	2–3 minutes	3–4 minutes

continued on page 182

VEGETABLES	FRESH COOKING TIME	FROZEN COOKING TIME
Green beans, whole	2–3 minutes	3–4 minutes
Greens, chopped	4–5 minutes	5–6 minutes
Leeks	2–3 minutes	3–4 minutes
Mixed vegetables	3–4 minutes	4–6 minutes
Okra	2–3 minutes	3–4 minutes
Onions, sliced	2–3 minutes	3–4 minutes
Parsnips, chunks	3–4 minutes	4–5 minutes
Peas, green	1–2 minutes	2–3 minutes
Peas, in the pod	1–2 minutes	2–3 minutes
Potatoes, cubed	3–4 minutes	4–5 minutes
Potatoes, large, whole	12–15 minutes	15–19 minutes
Potatoes, small, whole	8–10 minutes	12–14 minutes
Pumpkin, large pieces	8–10 minutes	10–14 minutes
Pumpkin, small pieces	4–5 minutes	6–7 minutes
Rutabaga, chunks	4–6 minutes	6–8 minutes
Rutabaga, slices	3–4 minutes	4–6 minutes
Spinach	1–2 minutes	2–3 minutes
Squash, acorn, slices	3–4 minutes	4–6 minutes
Squash, butternut squash, slices	4–6 minutes	6–8 minutes
Sweet potato, cubes	2–4 minutes	4–6 minutes
Sweet potato, large, whole	12–15 minutes	15–19 minutes
Sweet potato, small, whole	10–12 minutes	12–14 minutes
Tomatoes, quarters	2–3 minutes	4–5 minutes

FRUITS

When steaming fruit, you will need 1 cup (250 mL) of water and an ovenproof or steel bowl on a steam rack. Fresh or dried fruits are best steamed to preserve the texture and taste, as well as the vitamins and minerals. Steaming also retains the natural look of the fruit. Cook fruits of equal size and ripeness together.

FRUITS	FRESH COOKING TIME	DRIED COOKING TIME
Apples, slices or pieces	1–2 minutes	2–3 minutes
Apples, whole	3–4 minutes	4–6 minutes
Apricots, whole or halves	2–3 minutes	3–4 minutes
Peaches	2–3 minutes	4–5 minutes
Pears, slices or halves	2–3 minutes	4–5 minutes
Pears, whole	3–4 minutes	4–6 minutes
Plums	2–3 minutes	4–5 minutes
Raisins	n/a	4–5 minutes

Index

Library and Archives Canada Cataloguing in Publication

Haugen, Marilyn, author
    5-ingredient Instant Pot cookbook : 150 easy, quick & delicious recipes / Marilyn Haugen.

Includes index.
"Authorized by Instant Pot".
ISBN 978-0-7788-0608-0 (softcover)

    1. Pressure cooking. 2. Quick and easy cooking. 3. Cookbooks.
I. Title. II. Title: Five-ingredient Instant Pot cookbook.

TX840.P7H388 2018   641.5'87   C2018-903880-2